Alexia Marcelle Abegg

LIBERTYLOVE

25 Projects to Quilt & Sew Featuring Liberty of London Fabrics

stashBOOKS®

an imprint of C&T Publishing

Text copyright © 2013 by Alexia Abegg

Photography and Artwork copyright © 2013 by C&T Publishing, Inc.

Publisher: Amy Marson

Creative Director: Gailen Runge

Art Director/Book Designer: Kristy Zacharias

Editors: Lynn Koolish and Jill Mordick

Technical Editors: Alison M. Schmidt and Amanda Siegfried

Production Coordinator: Zinnia Heinzmann

Production Editors: S. Michele Fry and Joanna Burgarino

Photo Assistant: Cara Pardo

Illustrator: Alexia Abegg

Flat Quilt Photography by Christina Carty-Francis and Diane Pedersen of C&T Publishing, Inc., unless otherwise noted.

Style Photography by Alexia Abegg, unless otherwise noted.

Published by C&T Publishing, Inc., P.O. Box 1456, Lafayette, CA 94549

Library of Congress Cataloging-in-Publication Data

Abegg, Alexia Marcelle, 1980-

   Liberty love : 25 projects to quilt & sew featuring Liberty of London fabrics / Alexia Marcelle Abegg.

      pages cm

   Includes bibliographical references.

   ISBN 978-1-60705-626-3 (soft cover)

1. Patchwork--Patterns. 2. Quilting--Patterns. 3. Liberty of London, Inc. I. Title.

   TT835.A223 2013

   746.46'041--dc23

                        2012026457

Printed in China

10 9 8 7 6 5 4 3 2 1

DEDICATION

To my husband and family, without whom I would not have written this book. To my husband, Rob Bancroft, for your relentless support and encouragement. Thank you for all of those mornings you took care of everything because I like to write at night. I love you. To my parents, Jimmy and Michelle, for teaching me everything I know and for always pushing me to do my best and be creative. To my sisters, Pierrette and Jemina, and my mom, my sounding boards and creative critics, for helping me in every way to refine my ideas for the projects. To my mother-in-love, Dorothy, for your support and love.

ACKNOWLEDGMENTS

To Jemina, Pierrette, Michelle, Jude and Steve, Carrie, Anna, Robin, Katy, Stephanie, Kim, Rachel, Tim and Elizabeth, the Textile Fabric Store staff, City Quilter crew and teachers, and Harvey for your love, help, critique, and encouragement. To the C&T staff for helping to create the book I dreamed of. And last, to all of my friends, near and far, who have been a part of my journey as an artist, designer, and writer. I hope you know how much I appreciate you.

Thank you to Purl Soho for generously providing most of the Liberty of London fabrics for the book, to the Warm Company for providing Warm & White batting and Steam-A-Seam 2; to the people at Superbuzzy for their generosity; to Moda Fabrics, Andover Fabrics, and FreeSpirit Fabrics for providing fabrics for the book; and to Paper Pieces for providing the precut papers for English paper piecing the Queen Bee Tote Bag.

CONTENTS

PREFACE

I still remember my favorite blouse from the second grade. A simple, boat-necked, short-sleeved top, it was made from the softest Liberty of London Tana Lawn. The print was Wiltshire, with a soft, sky-at-night blue background and clusters of small berry-shaped flowers in shades of pink. I think it was that blouse that sparked my love not only for Liberty of London Tana Lawn fabric but also for the idea of one day sewing. The light and somehow soft, yet crisp, feel of the fabric and the watercolor look of the prints were a favorite even as a child.

I began collecting Liberty of London Tana Lawn as a girl on the verge of growing up and on the verge of making the step from sewing a little to realizing it was one of my life's true passions.

My first small patchwork project was a book cover. It was made with washed-out shades of blue Liberty my mom had given me, left over from Easter dresses she had sewn for my sisters and me. That simple little patchwork book cover cemented my relationship with sewing, and I haven't stopped, creating countless projects since.

My budding love of sewing only exponentially increased my love and fascination with Liberty prints. As a young adult I would go shopping in local fabric stores with my mom and sisters, and we would all ooh and aah over newly stocked rolls of Liberty, debating what to use them for and dreaming up all of the clothes we wanted to sew with them. To this day we all still have the same reaction.

I hope the projects in this book will make you dive into your Liberty stash, or rush out and buy your first yardage, and attack with sharp scissors and fresh inspiration!

And should we ever meet, I hope you will share your favorite print with me. Mine is Wiltshire, because of my favorite blouse from the second grade.

—Alexia

INTRODUCTION

The first few chapters of this book walk you through a small gallery of Liberty of London prints and provide some tips for combining Tana Lawn with other fabrics, as well as offering some sewing and quilting techniques.

I hope you will use the projects in this book as a starting point and put your own fingerprint on them. Make them your own, and bring your creativity to each and every one you sew.

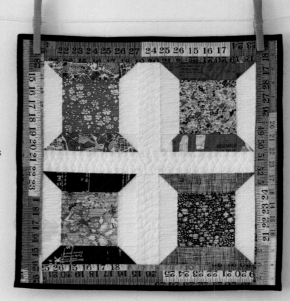

A Few Notes on Using the Patterns in This Book

If indicated by a pattern piece number, the pattern is included on the pattern sheets at the back of the book. Trace the required pieces in the desired size using pattern paper or template plastic. Be sure to transfer each and every mark on the pattern to your traced copy.

For pieces listed to cut with dimensions only, you can choose to create a pattern template with these measurements or to mark them directly onto the fabric, and then cut with scissors, or use a rotary cutter, ruler, and self-healing cutting mat.

For each of the projects—

- Liberty Tana Lawn yardage is calculated based on a fabric width of 54˝. For other fabric requirements, yardage assumes 44˝–45˝ fabrics, with usable width of 40˝. When laying out your pattern to cut, check, before cutting, that all of the pieces will fit in the way you have them arranged on the fabric.

- When using fusible interfacing and other fusible products, always refer to the manufacturer's instructions, which differ from product to product.

- Thread, hand-sewing needle, and basic tools required for each project are *not* included in individual lists of supplies. You will need thread for every project in the book except Liberty Bloom.

- As with any pattern, read the instructions from start to finish before beginning. I better understand the steps at the beginning of a project if I understand where I'm headed in later steps.

Liberty Art Fabrics releases two distinct and separate lines of prints every spring and fall: a seasonal collection and a classic collection. The seasonal collection is made up of new designs, some of which eventually become adopted as classics. The classic collection comprises classic designs in recurring, yet new, colorations. Let's have a look at a selection of prints from each group. Included are some old and some new, and many favorites I am sure you will recognize.

Prints designed in-house are marked as such. All other designs were created by outside artists or other unknown parties.

LIBERTY OF LONDON

A Gallery of Prints

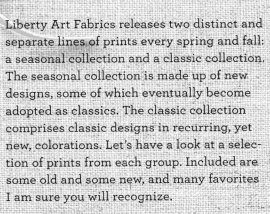

The range of prints created for the Liberty Art Fabrics seasonal collections is always forward thinking. Whether it is a classic floral redesigned or a new print by an artist, each print in the seasonal collections is always inspired— and inspiring. Because the seasonals are in print for a limited amount of time, they are all the more tempting to store away for an extra special project.

GNS

CLASSIC DESI

SEASONAL

1. *Tom's Jet*

2. *Flora Bo*

3. *Adelajda*

4. *Birdsong*

5. *Cars*

6. *Ella*

7. *Scotty's Tiger*

8. *Kyaoko*

9. *Natalie*
(*also known as Harriet*)

10. *Ashtead*

11. *Kelly*

12. *Unknown*

13. *Unknown*

CLASSIC DESIGNS

14. *Wiltshire, designed 1933, classic since 1979*

15. *Ianthe; designed 1967, unknown*

16. *Lola Weisselberg*

17. *Betsy, designed in-house 1933, classic since 1982*

18. *Thorpe, designed by the Hayward Studio 1968, classic since 1979*

19. *Poppy and Daisy, designed by the Jack Prince Studio 1974, classic since 1979*

20. *Edenham, designed 1994, classic since 1997*

21. *Tatum, designed 1955, classic since 2001*

22. *Fairford, designed in-house 2008, classic since 2011*

23. *Strawberry Thief, designed by William Morris 1883, classic since 1955*

24. *Felicite, designed 1933, classic since 2001*

25. *Millie, designed 2002, classic since 2006*

26. *Capel, printed 1978, classic since 1993*

27. *Glenjade, designed in-house 1930s, classic since 1979*

28. *Bourton, designed 1963, classic since 1987*

29. *Snug*

PAIRINGS

*Combining Liberty of London Tana Lawn
with Quilting and Fashion Fabrics*

MAKE THINGS EASIER
WHEN COMBINING FABRICS

You can easily combine different weights and types of fabrics with
Liberty of London Tana Lawn. As you read through some of the
projects in the book, you will see notes on the types of fabrics I have
selected. I frequently combine Liberty of London Tana Lawn with
other weights of fabrics. Through experimentation I have learned
how easy it is to combine them. Below are a few tips and special techniques that have worked in my sewing room.

- Prewash Tana Lawn so that the
  fabric becomes slightly less
  slippery and a little easier to
  handle. It is important when combining Tana Lawn with fabrics
  of a different weight or with a
  different fiber content to prewash
  not only the lawn but the other
  fabrics as well.

- If your project is primarily Tana
  Lawn and lightweight fabrics,
  use a size 70/10 sewing machine
  needle, universal or sharp. If you
  are combining Tana Lawn with
  heavier fabrics and interfacings,
  use a size 90/14 sharp needle.

Combining Liberty Tana lawn with a variety of fabrics

- If a project uses silk or sheer fabric in combination with Tana Lawn, use a lightweight cotton thread, such as Mettler fine embroidery or Aurifil cotton thread instead of polyester all-purpose thread (which is my usual choice for most sewing). I find that the cotton threads help the seams to lie flatter and press nicely, without puckering.

- If you want to beef up the Tana Lawn and make it stronger, thicker, and more stable for pairing with a heavier fabric, you can underline it with cotton voile, lawn, batiste, or muslin. Cut the exact same pieces from a lawn or batiste as from the Tana Lawn. Hand baste the underlining to the outer fabric's wrong side around the outer edges in the seam allowance. You can also add body with a fusible lightweight to midweight interfacing. I like Bi-Stretch Lite by Pellon, Shape-Flex, and French Fuse interfacing.

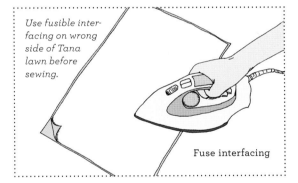

Use fusible interfacing on wrong side of Tana lawn before sewing.

Fuse interfacing

- If you are getting show-through when making lined garments, you can underline the Tana Lawn before sewing following the directions above.

- For quilts with lighter-colored Tana Lawn in combination with regular quilting cotton, press seams toward the quilting cotton to prevent the seams from showing through the lightweight Liberty fabric.

- When quilting with Tana Lawn, I like to starch my fabrics first. This gives them a little more tooth, to grab and stick to the other fabrics, as well as keeping things stiff for lining up seams precisely.

- Last, on creative combinations of fabrics, be adventurous. When embarking on a new project, the first and most exciting step, or the most daunting, can be selecting fabrics. I think you will see that it is possible to combine Liberty of London prints with new and current fabrics from quilting and fashion to achieve many different looks. From edgy and fashion forward to soft and pretty, the Liberty prints can be enhanced and transformed by the fabrics with which you pair them.

Be adventurous!

TOOLS, TIPS, AND TECHNIQUES

for Sewing and Quilting

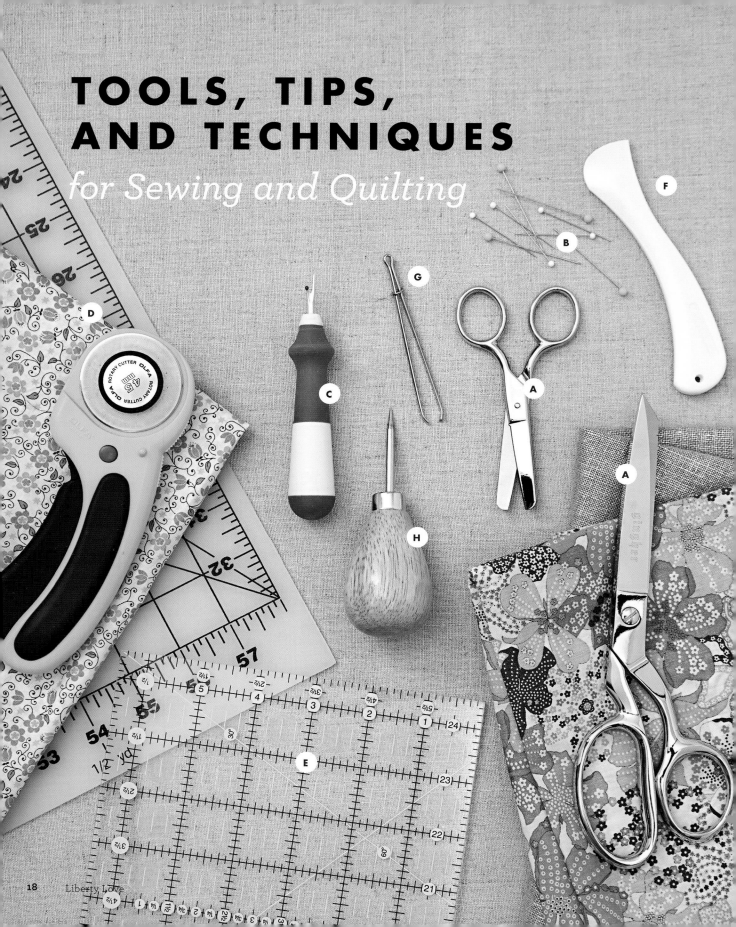

TOOLS AND SUPPLIES

These are some essential tools to have on hand. I have included my favorite and most-used items.

A. Scissors

I use my 8″ Gingher knife-edge scissors for cutting almost everything, including patterns. They can be easily sharpened and, with care, will last indefinitely. I use embroidery scissors for precise cutting in small areas. I use small blunt-end scissors for clipping and notching seam allowances and trimming threads because the tip of the scissor is easy to see and is nice and sharp right to the end. Even if you have them in your pocket they won't poke through, so they are great for travel and handwork on the go.

B. Pins

For light- to midweight fabrics I use thin glass-head pins. For mid- to heavyweight fabrics, I use long yellow plastic ball-head pins that are sharp but a little thicker.

C. Seam Ripper

A seam ripper with a thin point and a sharp cutter is essential. It will glide through stitches, helping to keep your fabric intact when ripping out mistakes.

D. Rotary Cutter and Self-Healing Mat

I like to use an ergonomic cutter with a 45mm-blade and as large a mat as I can fit in my sewing space.

E. Rotary Cutting Rulers

A 6″ × 24″ ruler with 30°, 45°, and 60° lines is the most useful because it can reach the span of a 44″–45″ fabric folded in half selvage to selvage for cutting. It allows you to cut across the fabric in one motion. The 45° mark on the ruler works well to cut bias. The 30° and 60° marks are great for marking quilting lines in a diamond grid.

F. Hera Marker

A Hera marker is a plastic tool for marking quilting lines. It creases the fabric to mark and is therefore foolproof because you know it will always wash out!

G. Bodkin

A bodkin is a tool that attaches to the end of elastic, ribbon, or draw cord to feed it through a casing.

H. Awl

To aid in guiding fabric while sewing, for punching holes, and for many other applications, a pointed-tip awl is quite handy.

I. Fabric Markers

Blue wash-away markers make a nice vivid mark on light fabrics.

J. Chalk Pencils

The most all-purpose marking tool, chalk pencils wash away or brush off and are good for marking notches and other important pattern markings.

K. Tracing Wheel and Transfer Paper

Use these for garment sewing when marking interior placement lines, darts, seamlines, and more.

L. Rulers

I keep two essential rulers on hand: a 1˝ × 6˝ red gridded C-Thru ruler for checking seam allowances, hems, and machine needle position and an 2˝ × 18˝ red gridded C-Thru ruler for marking patterns on fabric, measuring larger pieces, and drafting patterns.

Iron and Ironing Board

Learn to love your iron; pressed seams make a sewn item look professional and finished. I like adjustable steam; when pressing quilt blocks I turn off or lower steam to prevent stretching pieces.

M. Press Cloth

When pressing fine fabrics, a press cloth protects them from the iron. When using fusibles, use a press cloth to protect your fabric, iron, and ironing board from any residue.

N. Pattern Paper

Similar to lightweight interfacing, pattern tracing paper is slightly sheer and fairly durable.

O. Template Plastic

To make patterns for cutting quilt pieces, trace the cutting lines, stitching lines, pattern piece information, and any matching symbols onto the plastic and cut it out. The template can then be traced onto the wrong side of the fabric with a pencil or chalk.

P. Measuring Tape

Whether measuring a person or a quilt, a flexible measuring tape is key.

Q. Hand-Sewing Needles

I use sharps for most tasks. For quilting with perle cotton, try a crewel needle, going up in size to correlate with the thickness of the thread.

R. Thimble

A nice leather thimble will save your fingers when quilting or hand sewing. I like to use a Clover coin thimble. It is comfortable and easy to get used to wearing.

SEWING TIPS

Preparation

- Prewash fabrics whenever possible, except when you do not plan to wash the item after finishing it.

  FOR BAGS AND ACCESSORIES: I like to preserve the original finish of the fabric as it comes from the manufacturer, so I do not prewash.

  WHEN WORKING WITH PRECUTS: Lightly spritz with water and press precuts with a high steam setting to preshrink rather than washing.

- Always iron your fabrics to remove any creases or wrinkles before cutting.

Cutting

- When preparing fabric for cutting, unless otherwise indicated, fold the fabric in half lengthwise with the woven, selvage edges together and the wrong sides of the fabric facing each other.

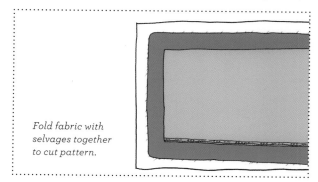

Fold fabric with selvages together to cut pattern.

- Place pattern pieces marked "on the fold" on the center folded line of the fabric and do not cut through the fold.

- When cutting, keep all of the fabric on the cutting table. When fabric hangs off the edges it can stretch out of place as you cut.

- When using a paper pattern, cut both the traced pattern paper copy and the fabric layered together, rather than trimming the traced pattern first—you'll get a more accurate result.

STAYSTITCHING

Staystitch areas that will get clipped or notched. Before sewing the seam, sew a line of stitching just outside of (closer to the raw edge than) where your final seamline will be. This will keep the clipped area from extending beyond the seamline.

FINISHING SEAMS

If your item will not be lined or will have seams exposed to wear and tear, it is a good idea to finish the seams. To do so, either of two easy techniques can be completed on a regular sewing machine:

- For the easiest seam finish, sew a second row of straight stitching a scant ⅛˝ outside of the seam stitching line and then trim away the excess seam allowance.

- Or use a zigzag stitch to finish the edges of the cut pattern pieces separately before sewing them together. Remember you only need to finish edges that will not be hemmed or trapped inside another seam.

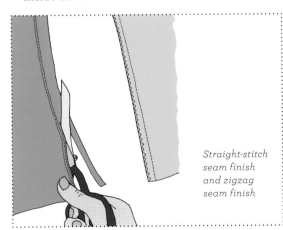

Straight-stitch seam finish and zigzag seam finish

After you have sewn the seams, clip and notch any curved edges so that they will lie flat when the seam is turned right side out. Cut away excess seam allowances at corners as well.

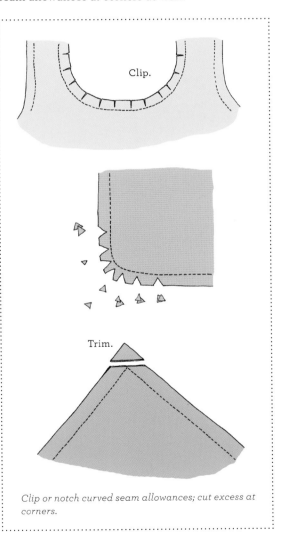

Clip or notch curved seam allowances; cut excess at corners.

With bulky seams, you can trim the seam allowances in half, parallel to the raw edge, to reduce bulk.

INVISIBLE ZIPPER

Of the many ways to sew an invisible zipper, the following is the method I prefer.

1. Use your machine's zipper foot. Refer to your machine manual for zipper foot instructions. Many zipper feet can be used in either a right or left position. Use the foot to sew close to the plastic coils of the invisible zipper.

2. Sew the seam where the zipper will be placed from the hem to the zipper stop point.

3. Mark the zipper from the upper cut edge of the tape down to the length of the opening and make a mark on the wrong side of the zipper tape.

4. Place the zipper right sides together with the zipper seamline. To do so, place the garment wrong side out with the opening facing you, and roll the seam allowances to the inside as if you had already sewn the entire back seam. Place the right side of the zipper against the right side of the seam allowances that are showing.

5. Temporarily pin the zipper to the seam allowances. Stop pinning 4˝ from the zipper stop point at the bottom of the zipper. This will help keep the zipper from twisting when sewn in steps 6–7.

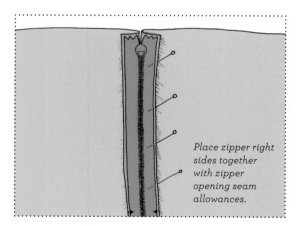

Place zipper right sides together with zipper opening seam allowances.

6. Unzip the zipper and sew a seam with one side of the zipper and the same side opening. Stop sewing at the mark and backstitch.

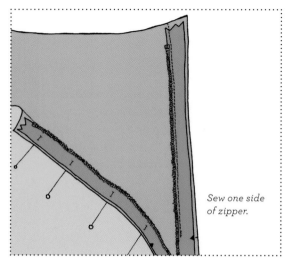

Sew one side of zipper.

7. Without twisting the zipper, sew the remaining side of the zipper right sides together with the remaining zipper opening edge.

8. Pull the zipper head up through the seam and zip up the zipper.

9. Press the seam flat from the outside.

10. If the tail of the zipper is much longer than the zipper stop point, shorten the zipper: Set your machine to the widest zigzag stitch with the stitch length set to zero. Place the zipper under the presser foot and stitch a bar tack across the coils of the zipper. Cut away the excess, leaving about ¼˝ below the bar tack.

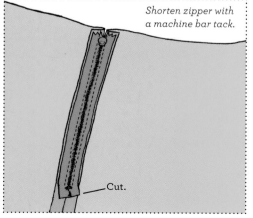

Shorten zipper with a machine bar tack.

Cut.

SEWING STRAIGHT TO CURVED EDGES

1. Staystitch (page 23) the seamline of the straight piece.

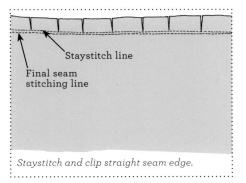

Staystitch and clip straight seam edge.

2. Clip into the seam allowance not quite to the seamline in the section of the straight piece that needs to go around the curve.

3. Pin in place, spreading the clipped sections apart. The straight piece will now conform to the curved edge of the other fabric piece.

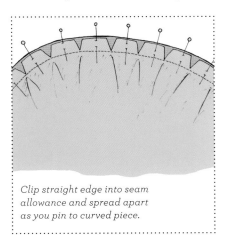

Clip straight edge into seam allowance and spread apart as you pin to curved piece.

BOX-SHAPED ITEMS WITH FRONT, BACK, SIDE, AND BOTTOM SEAMS INTERSECTING

For items such as the Queen Bee Tote Bag (page 117) that have a box shape, the corners need special consideration.

1. Mark a dot, the seam allowance distance away from the edges, at the corner of each of the pieces that will be sewn to create a finished box-shaped corner.

2. As you sew each seam, stop sewing at the corner dot and backstitch. This will allow each of the fabrics to get sewn to the same point, without sewing over previous seams.

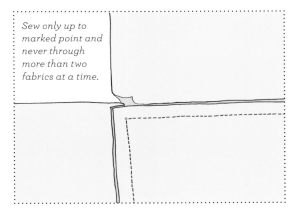

Sew only up to marked point and never through more than two fabrics at a time.

3. Each of the three seams that create a finished corner is sewn separately and up to the point.

4. Before turning the bag right side out, trim away the excess seam allowances at the corner.

SLIP STITCH

I use the slip stitch for most hand-sewn hems and for hand finishing binding.

1. Knot the thread end and bring the needle through one of the folded edges you will be sewing.

2. Pick up a thread or two of the opposite side fabric at the same point, sew into the fold, and repeat.

LADDER STITCH

I use the ladder stitch to hand sew seams closed.

1. Knot the thread end and bring the needle through one of the folded edges you will be sewing.

2. Take a ⅛˝-long stitch in the opposite side fold, entering the fabric at the same point where you just exited the opposite side fold, and repeat.

The stitch makes little rungs of a ladder between the two folded edges of the fabric as you go back and forth. When you tighten the stitches, they should be nearly invisible.

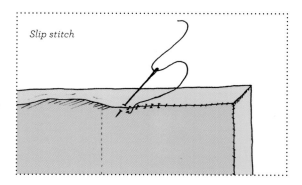
Slip stitch

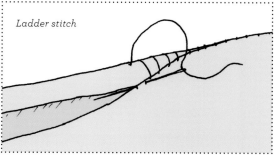
Ladder stitch

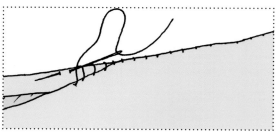

QUILTING TIPS

Rotary Cutting

To rotary cut fabric:

1. Fold the fabric as described in Cutting (page 22), and place the 6˝ × 24˝ ruler on the fabric with the long edge of the ruler parallel to the raw edge and the short edge of the ruler parallel to the fold of the fabric. The goal is for the edge you will cut to form a 90° angle with the fold of the fabric. Hold the rotary cutter in your dominant hand and always cut on the same side of the ruler as your dominant hand. Use the other hand to hold the ruler firmly in place.

2. Glide the blade along the edge of the ruler, keeping your fingers on the ruler as far away from the blade as possible, pressing down and away from you to cut the fabric.

3. Make one cut to square up the fabric. Unfold the fabric to make sure the cut edge is straight. If you see a V, refold and cut again.

4. After you have made the first cut, turn the fabric around so that the ruler is measuring into the yardage the amount you need to cut.

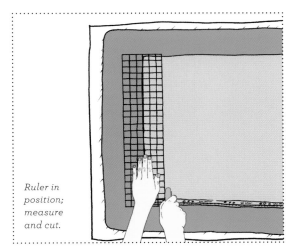

Ruler in position; measure and cut.

5. You can cut fabric into strips the width you need, and subcut these into smaller pieces such as squares and rectangles.

Cutting with Scissors

If you prefer to cut your fabrics for piecing with scissors:

1. Trace the template pattern (or measure and draw squares or rectangles) onto template plastic.

2. Cut out the templates with scissors on the cutting lines.

3. Trace each template onto the wrong side of the fabric using a mechanical pencil.

4. Cut each traced piece on the drawn line with scissors.

Using a Design Wall for Quilt Layout

Using a design wall or flat surface, arrange all of the blocks that will make up your quilt. Play with the placement of the fabrics until you are happy with each block. I like to take a quick photo to remember the placement of each fabric.

Sewing

Accurate ¼˝ seams are key in quilting. If you are having a hard time sewing a true ¼˝ with your regular sewing machine foot, you may want to invest in a ¼˝ foot with a guide on it to keep your fabric in line as you sew.

When pinning seams that need to align, I like to pin just next to the seamline on either side, never through the actual stitching. Pressing the seam allowances in advance in alternating directions helps the seams nest together more easily for exact alignment.

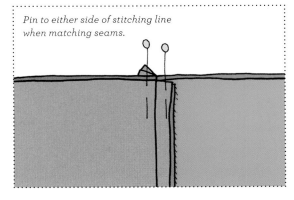

Pin to either side of stitching line when matching seams.

Pressing your seams and blocks when quilting is vital to creating beautiful and accurate quilts. I like to press seams open and then in the direction indicated by the pattern at every stage of creating a quilt. Without pressing, fabrics can shift and bunch, or a quilt block may appear to be smaller than it actually is.

When quilting, rather than ironing as most of us are accustomed to—moving the iron side to side, pressing with all of your might as you remove the wrinkles from a cotton shirt—it is important to press instead. Pressing is a gentle use of the iron, lowering the iron flat onto the area to be pressed, using a small amount of pressure without moving the iron side to side, lifting straight up when ready to move to another section, and again lowering flat onto the fabric to be pressed.

Preparing the Quilt for Quilting

I add 4˝ to the height and width of any quilt top for the batting and backing size, but I quilt my own quilts on a domestic machine. If you plan to have your quilt quilted on a longarm quilting machine, refer to the requirements of your quilter or the machine when purchasing backing and batting.

1. Trim the selvages from the backing fabric.

2. I like to piece my backing with a vertical seam (just like the center back seam in a garment). Cut the backing fabric into pieces the same length as the batting. To create a backing wide enough for the size of the quilt you are making, sew the two (or more if needed) pieces of fabric together lengthwise. Be sure to allow extra yardage if you want to match a repeat in the fabric print.

3. Press the quilt top, batting, and backing before basting them together.

4. Place the backing fabric onto a flat surface with the wrong side up. Tape the corners using painter's tape to secure.

5. Place the quilt batting onto the backing and smooth.

6. Place the quilt top onto the batting with the wrong side facing the batting. Match the center of the quilt with the center of the backing at the top and bottom edges.

PIN BASTING

To pin baste, use small, curved quilter's safety pins and pin through all of the layers of the quilt in a 4˝–6˝ grid.

SPRAY BASTING

Spray basting is done with an adhesive quilt basting spray.

1. Fold back the quilt top halfway and spray the surface of the batting with the spray according to the manufacturer's instructions.

2. Fold the quilt top back over the sprayed batting and smooth. Repeat with the other half of the quilt top.

3. Fold up the batting and quilt top together and spray the backing fabric in the same fashion. Fold down the quilt top and smooth. Repeat with the other half of the quilt.

Quilting

STRAIGHT-LINE QUILTING

For straight-line quilting, it is essential to use a walking foot on your sewing machine. To mark lines for quilting, use either a wash-away marker or a Hera marker. Use a ruler to keep the lines straight.

Stitch each quilting line, pivoting at corners if necessary. Leave long thread tails at the beginning and end of every stitching line that begins or ends within the quilt top. After quilting, thread the tails onto a hand-sewing needle, bury them in the batting layer of the quilt, and trim away excess. For stitching lines that begin and end at the very edges of the quilt, backstitch at the beginning and end and trim away excess thread.

FREE-MOTION QUILTING

To free-motion quilt, choose a design you like and adjust your machine for free-motion sewing according to the manufacturer's instructions. This should include changing the foot to a free-motion or darning foot and usually involves dropping the feed dogs.

To free-motion quilt you will move the quilt top to "draw" on the quilt with the thread and needle, as if you were drawing on a piece of paper by moving the piece of paper rather than the pencil. As with straight-line quilting, your threads will need to be either buried in the batting or backstitched at the edges of the quilt.

Below are a few of my favorite designs for free-motion quilting.

Loopy

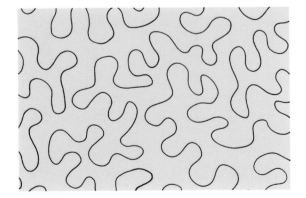

Stipple

Zigzag image:

Zigzag

Binding

Binding is used to finish the edges of quilts. (It can also be used to finish the edges of bags, accessories, and clothing.) If the quilt has curved edges, such as scallops, use bias binding. If the edges of the quilt are straight, use straight-cut binding.

CUTTING BIAS BINDING STRIPS

1. Place the fabric in a single layer on the cutting mat. Place the 45° mark of a 6″ × 24″ ruler in line with the selvage edge, extending from the selvage edge to the cut edge of the fabric.

2. Cut along the edge of the ruler for the entire width of the fabric. Do not move the ruler while completing the first cut (Figure A).

3. Place a piece on top of the other, aligning the cut edges (Figure B).

4. Fold the fabrics toward you so that the cut edges remain aligned and the width of the fabrics will fit under the 24″ length of the ruler (Figure C).

5. Using the rotary cutter and ruler, cut the fabric into 2¼″ strips until you have enough binding plus 10″ to go all the way around the quilt.

Over the years I have determined the approximate amounts I need based on quilt size, and I do not like to cut bias binding from less than ⅓ yard of fabric. I usually buy ½ yard because I would rather have fewer seams in my binding and extra fabric in my stash. Working with the minimum amount of fabric will increase the number of seams needed in the binding.

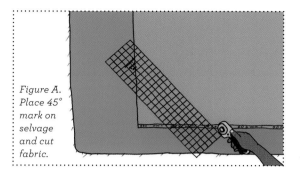

Figure A. Place 45° mark on selvage and cut fabric.

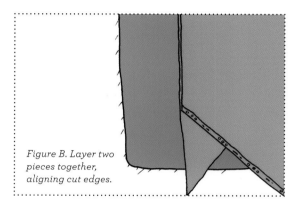

Figure B. Layer two pieces together, aligning cut edges.

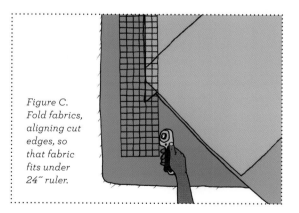

Figure C. Fold fabrics, aligning cut edges, so that fabric fits under 24″ ruler.

CUTTING STRAIGHT BINDING STRIPS

Cut strips 2¼˝ × width of fabric, using a rotary cutter and ruler, until you have enough binding to go all the way around the quilt and have about 10˝ left over. Remember you will lose ½˝ of each strip to the seam allowances.

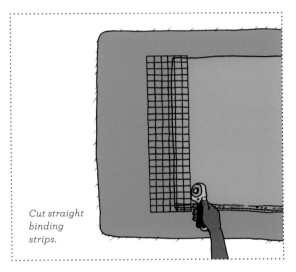

Cut straight binding strips.

MAKING CONTINUOUS BINDING

To join the ends of the binding strips:

1. Overlap the ends of the binding strips, with right sides together in a 90° angle.

2. Sew across the fabrics at a 45° angle.

3. Trim the seam allowance to ¼˝. This seam type will create the least-bulky seams in the binding.

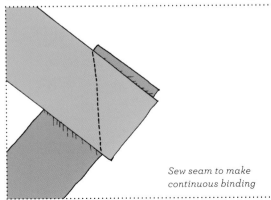

Sew seam to make continuous binding

APPLYING THE BINDING

To bind the quilt:

1. Fold the joined binding in half lengthwise, wrong sides together, and press.

2. Leaving about 10˝ excess at the beginning, start in the middle of one of the side edges. Align the raw edges of the binding with the outer edge of the quilt and sew the binding to the front of the quilt using a ¼˝ seam allowance.

> **TIP** *I usually do not pin the binding to the quilt because the binding can give as you sew it in place, creating puckers or bubbles in the seam. However, you might want to preview the binding by placing it around the edges before you start sewing to make sure that none of the binding seams will be at a corner.*

3. When you come to a corner, stop sewing ¼˝ from the quilt's edge and backstitch.

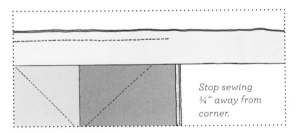

Stop sewing ¼˝ away from corner.

4. Turn the quilt so that the unsewn edge of the quilt is ready to go under the needle. Fold the binding back away from you, making a 45° angle, and pin it in place.

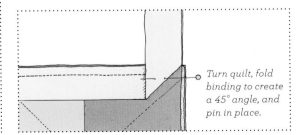

Turn quilt, fold binding to create a 45° angle, and pin in place.

5. Fold the binding back toward you, aligning the fold with the upper edge of the quilt, and pin in place.

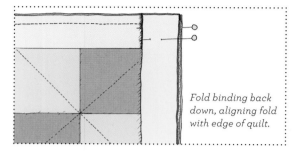

Fold binding back down, aligning fold with edge of quilt.

6. Sew from the upper edge over the mitered binding and down the length of the quilt using the same ¼˝ seam allowance.

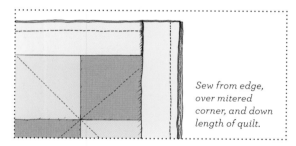

Sew from edge, over mitered corner, and down length of quilt.

7. Repeat this mitering step at each corner of the binding. Stop sewing about 10˝ before the beginning of your binding seam.

FINISHING THE BINDING

1. Overlap the binding tails smoothly along the quilt edge and trim the overlap to 2¼˝.

2. Unfold each end of the binding strip. Pin the ends right sides together with the cut edges aligned in the same 90° shape as when joining binding strips. Sew across the strips from corner to corner at a 45° angle.

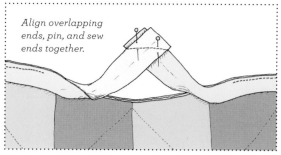

Align overlapping ends, pin, and sew ends together.

3. Trim the seam allowance to ¼˝ and press the seam open.

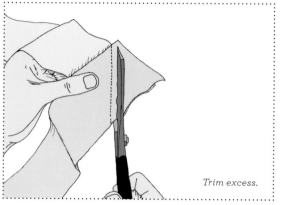

Trim excess.

4. Refold the binding and sew it onto the front of the quilt in the same fashion as you sewed the binding previously.

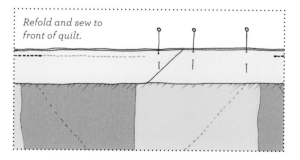

Refold and sew to front of quilt.

5. Wrap the binding around to the back of the quilt and hand sew in place using the slip stitch (page 26).

See the Resources section (page 159) for a list of my favorite quilting and how-to-sew books with more information on sewing and quilting basics.

QUILTS
FOR
LITTLE
AND BIG

NINE-PATCH REVISITED BABY QUILT

NINE-PATCH REVISITED BABY QUILT

FINISHED BLOCK SIZE: 12″ × 12″

FINISHED SIZE: 36″ × 36″

Inspired by the clean lines and simplicity of a traditional Nine-Patch quilt block, this uncomplicated baby quilt is quick and easy to sew. Its small size is perfect for tossing over a stroller or baby carrier. I can just see it made up of sweet pinks or baby boy blues for the perfect baby gift, sure to become a beloved and worn security blanket.

The nine blocks in the quilt consist of four different aqua tonal Liberty of London fabrics, one coordinating aqua cotton print, and a solid gray fabric. I chose a classic diamond grid for the machine quilting and used a soft gray machine quilting thread that blended with the fabrics.

Supplies Needed

The fabrics shown here, paired with the Liberty of London Tana Lawn prints, are all woven, quilting weight, and 100% cotton.

⅜ yard (or 1 fat quarter) each of 4 different aqua Liberty Tana Lawn prints for blocks

⅜ yard (or 1 fat quarter) aqua print for center block

¾ yard gray solid for corner blocks

1¼ yards backing fabric

⅓ yard binding fabric

Batting: 40″ × 40″

Hera marker

24″-long quilting ruler with 30° marking

Cutting

Tana Lawn and Cotton Prints

Cut 1 square 12½″ × 12½″ from each fabric for a total of 5 squares.

Solid Cotton

Cut 4 squares 12½″ × 12½″.

Binding

Cut 4 strips 2¼″ × width of fabric.

CONSTRUCTION

Unless otherwise indicated, use a ¼˝ seam allowance and sew all seams with the right sides of the fabric facing each other.

Sew

1. Arrange the blocks as shown in the finished quilt photo (page 37). Sew 3 blocks together to complete the first row.

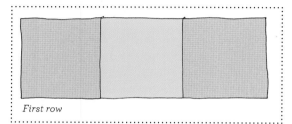

First row

2. Sew the remaining blocks together to complete 2 more rows.

3. Press the seam allowances of the rows in alternating directions.

Assemble

1. Working from top to bottom, and referring to the finished quilt photo (page 37) for the layout, sew the 3 rows together, nesting the seam allowances to help keep the seams aligned.

2. Press the seam allowances toward the lower edge of the quilt.

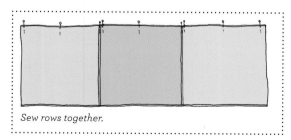

Sew rows together.

Finish

Refer to Quilting Tips (pages 26–32) for quilting and finishing.

1. Layer the quilt top, batting, and backing.

2. Baste the quilt to prepare for quilting.

3. Machine quilt using straight-line quilting spaced 2˝ apart in a diamond grid (see below).

4. Square up if needed and bind the quilt.

DIAMOND GRID INSTRUCTIONS

1. Align the 30° line of a 24˝ quilting ruler with a vertical block seam.

2. Mark along the long edge of the ruler using the Hera marker. Slide the ruler so that half of the ruler is still aligned with the mark you just made and extend the line so that it runs the length of the quilt top.

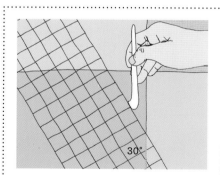

Align 30° line with vertical block seam and complete first diagonal mark on quilt top.

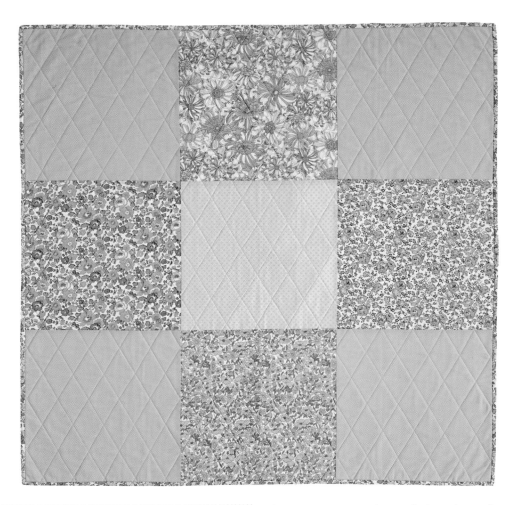

3. Mark the next quilting row in the same fashion, 2˝ away from the first. Repeat until you have covered the entire width of the quilt top with lines 2˝ apart.

4. Repeat Steps 1–3 but with the ruler in the opposite direction to complete the diamond quilting grid. Use either the opposite 30° line on the straight seamlines or the 60° line on the marked line from Step 3.

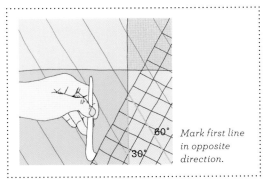

Mark first line in opposite direction.

SIXTEEN-PATCH
POSTAGE STAMP
BABY QUILT

SIXTEEN-PATCH POSTAGE STAMP BABY QUILT

FINISHED BLOCK SIZE: 8˝ × 8˝

FINISHED SIZE: 40˝ × 48˝

I designed this baby quilt hoping to create something that is simple enough for the busy sewer to make yet has that special quality that makes a quilt become a family heirloom. This quilt combines Sixteen-Patch quilt blocks, made with twenty different Liberty of London fabrics, and solid blocks, using Japanese cotton double gauze in soft gray with off-white, painterly dots, designed by Naomi Ito.

In keeping with the vintage style, I hand quilted, using a perle cotton in size 8, in a diamond grid that intersects the corners of each block.

Supplies Needed

With the exception of the 100% cotton double gauze fabric used for the solid blocks in the quilt top, the fabrics shown here are Liberty of London Tana Lawn prints.

20 different 8˝ × 12˝ pieces of Liberty Tana Lawn in a variety of colors for Sixteen-Patch blocks

1 yard cotton double gauze for setting squares

1⅝ yards backing fabric*

⅜ yard binding fabric

Batting: 44˝ × 52˝

Perle cotton size 8 for hand quilting

Crewel needle size 4 (preferably with a large eye)

* Requires 44˝-wide fabric. If yours is narrower, you will need additional yardage to piece the backing.

Cutting

Tana Lawn Prints
   Cut 12 squares 2½˝ × 2½˝ from each fabric for sixteen-patches.

Double Gauze Print
   Cut 15 squares 8½˝ × 8½˝ for setting squares.

Binding
   Cut 6 strips 2¼˝ × width of fabric.

CONSTRUCTION

Unless otherwise indicated, use a ¼˝ seam allowance and sew all seams with the right sides of the fabric facing each other.

Sew

SIXTEEN-PATCH BLOCKS

1. Sew 4 Tana Lawn 2½˝ × 2½˝ squares together into a row. Press all seam allowances in the row to the same side.

Complete row of 4 squares

2. Repeat Step 1 to make 4 separate rows of 4 squares each, pressing the seam allowances of rows in alternating directions.

3. Sew the 4 rows together, nesting the seam allowances to help align the seams to create the Sixteen-Patch block.

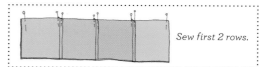

Sew first 2 rows.

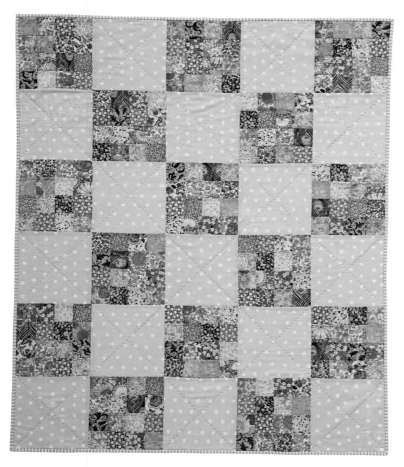

4. Press the seam allowances of each row down toward the lower edge of the block.

5. Repeat Steps 1–3 with the remaining 2½˝ × 2½˝ squares to complete all 15 Sixteen-Patch blocks.

Assemble

1. Sew 3 Tana Lawn Sixteen-Patch blocks and 2 double-gauze 8½˝ × 8½˝ squares together from left to right into a row, beginning and ending with a Sixteen-Patch block. Press all the seam allowances to the same side. Repeat this step to make 3 more rows with the same block layout.

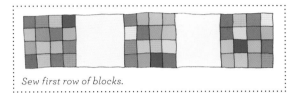

Sew first row of blocks.

2. Sew 3 double-gauze 8½˝ × 8½˝ squares and 2 Tana Lawn Sixteen-Patch blocks together from left to right into a row, beginning and ending with 8½˝ × 8½˝ squares. Press the seam allowances in this row in the opposite direction of the previous rows. Repeat this step to make 3 more rows with the same block layout.

3. Working from top to bottom and referring to the finished quilt photo (page 40) for the layout, sew the rows together to complete the quilt top. Press the seam allowances down toward the lower edge of the quilt.

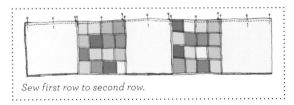

Sew first row to second row.

Finish

Refer to Quilting Tips (pages 26–32) for quilting and finishing.

1. Layer the quilt top, batting, and backing.

2. Baste the quilt to prepare for quilting.

3. Hand quilt using straight-line quilting in a diamond grid (see below) that bisects the corners of each Sixteen-Patch block or setting square.

DIAMOND GRID INSTRUCTIONS

1. Use a quilting ruler and Hera marker to mark the quilting lines from corner to corner of each setting square or Sixteen-Patch block, extending the lines to cover the entire quilt top. Mark all right-leaning as well as left-leaning lines to complete the grid.

Hand quilting with perle cotton

2. Square up if needed and then bind the quilt.

SEASHORE BABY QUILT

FINISHED SIZE: 38¼˝ × 60˝

This French-inspired baby quilt in red, white, gray, and blue has rows of scallop-shaped appliqués, reminiscent of café awnings and beach umbrellas. If you have never tried machine appliqué, I encourage you to give this quilt a try. A special technique using lightweight fusible interfacing makes the appliqué very easy.

This quilt combines two different blue Liberty of London fabrics, two different polka dot fabrics, and a subtle white print background fabric with soft pin dots. I chose to machine quilt this quilt in straight, vertical rows, spaced 1˝ apart, echoing the style of a striped awning.

Supplies Needed

The fabrics shown here, paired with the Liberty Tana Lawn prints, are all woven, quilting weight, and 100% cotton.

¼ yard each of 2 different blue Liberty Tana Lawn prints for appliqués

½ yard red-and-white dot print for appliqués

½ yard gray-and-white dot print for appliqués

2 yards subtle white print for background

2 yards backing fabric

½ yard binding fabric

3½ yards lightweight fusible interfacing (20˝ wide)

Batting: 43˝ × 64˝

Silicone Release Paper (C&T Publishing) or appliqué pressing sheet

Cutting

Template patterns are on tissue paper pattern sheets.

Tana Lawn Prints

Cut 1 of pattern piece 2A from each fabric.

Dot Prints

Cut 2 of pattern piece 2A from each fabric.

White Print Background

Cut 6 pieces 10½˝ × width of fabric.

Lightweight Fusible Interfacing

Cut 6 of pattern piece 2A.

Note: Lightweight fusible interfacing is usually 20˝ wide, which is too narrow to fit piece 2A across the width. When cutting piece 2A out of the interfacing, place the pattern piece lengthwise.

Binding

Cut 6 strips 2¼˝ × width of fabric.

CONSTRUCTION

Unless otherwise indicated, use a ¼˝ seam allowance and sew all seams with the right sides of the fabric facing each other.

Sew

SCALLOP APPLIQUÉ BLOCKS

1. Sew the scallop edges of a cotton print piece and a fusible interfacing piece together with the right side of the fabric facing the fusible side of the interfacing.

> **TIP** *Mark the point of the stitching line, between each scallop, onto your fabric using a fabric marker or chalk. As you sew, when you reach each marked point, stop, lower the needle down into the point of the seam, raise the presser foot, pivot, lower the presser foot, and continue sewing. This will ensure that you get nice crisp points between the scallops.*

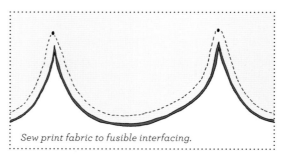

Sew print fabric to fusible interfacing.

2. Clip the seam allowances along the scallop edges and clip into each small corner of the seam allowance where the scallops meet.

Clip seam allowances.

3. Turn the appliqué right side out. The fusible side of the interfacing should be facing you when you are looking at the back of the appliqué.

4. Press the pieces of appliqué on the fabric side, using the Silicone Release Paper or an appliqué pressing sheet between the fusible interfacing and the ironing board.

5. Repeat Steps 1–4 to complete all of the scallop appliqués.

6. Fuse an appliqué piece, centered across the width of the fabric, to a background piece, aligning upper raw edges and with the interfacing toward the background fabric. It will gently adhere.

Fuse appliqué in place on background fabric.

Note: From this point forward, handle the blocks gently. If the appliqué comes up from the background fabric, just give it another press to fuse it in place.

7. Stitch the scallop edge of the appliqué to the background fabric by machine.

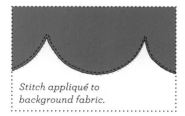

Stitch appliqué to background fabric.

8. Repeat Steps 6 and 7 with each of the remaining appliqués and background fabric pieces.

Assemble

Follow the photo of the quilt (page 45) for color placement. Working from top to bottom, sew the rows together. Press. Trim the sides of the quilt top even with the sides of the scallop appliqué.

Finish

Refer to Quilting Tips (pages 26–32) for quilting and finishing.

1. Layer the quilt top, batting, and backing.

2. Baste the quilt to prepare for quilting.

3. Machine quilt using straight-line quilting in vertical rows spaced 1˝ apart.

4. Square up if needed and bind the quilt.

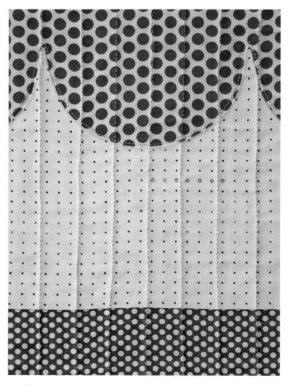

Quilting in 1˝ vertical rows

This quilt is ready for a trip to the beach!

GOODNIGHT
FAIRY TALE
QUILT

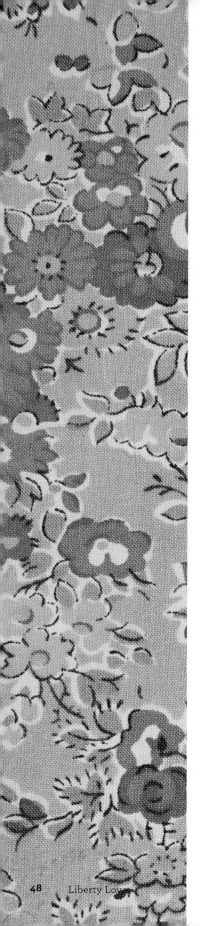

GOODNIGHT FAIRY TALE QUILT

FINISHED BLOCK SIZE: 10˝ × 10˝

FINISHED SIZE (AS SHOWN): 40˝ × 50˝

For twin size (70˝ × 90˝), refer to materials and cutting information on page 50.

This whimsical quilt's simple style leaves plenty of room for the fabrics to dictate the overall look. Made up in soft pinks, greens, and shades of aqua with a cream background fabric, this quilt would be perfect for a little girl still reading fairy tales. The curved piecing is not as hard as it looks, and this quilt comes together quite quickly.

To highlight the simple style, I free-motion quilted in a loopy, allover design.

Supplies Needed

The fabrics shown here, paired with the Liberty Tana Lawn prints, are all woven, quilting weight and voile, and 100% cotton.

20 different 8˝ × 8˝ pieces of cotton fabrics in a variety of colors for saucer centers

1¼ yards each cream cotton with blue dots and cream cotton with strawberry print for background squares

1⅝ yards* backing fabric

½ yard binding fabric

Batting: 44˝ × 54˝

* Requires minimum 44˝ usable width of fabric. If your fabric is narrower, you will need additional yardage to piece the backing.

Cutting

Template patterns are on tissue paper pattern sheets.

T I P *If you are using a directional print, like a stripe or the mushroom print in this quilt, fold the fabric wrong sides together and first cut 2 of template 4A printed side up, with the curved edge oriented to the top of the design, as if you are looking at one of the upper quarter circles on a finished block. Next, cut 2 of template 4A printed side up with the curved edge down, as if you are looking at one of the lower quarter circles on a finished block. This will give you four pieces with the print all oriented in the correct direction. Lay out and sew the block carefully to keep the print direction correct.*

Cutting, continued

Tana Lawn and Cotton Prints

Cut 4 of template piece 4A from each of the 20 fabrics for the saucer centers.

Background Fabric

Cut 40 of template piece 5A from each of the background fabrics for the block backgrounds.

Binding Fabric

Cut 5 strips 2¼˝ × width of fabric.

CONSTRUCTION

Unless otherwise indicated, use a ¼˝ seam allowance and sew all seams with the right sides of the fabric facing each other.

Sew

SAUCER BLOCKS

1. Beginning with 1 saucer center piece and 1 background piece, fold and crease each piece in half through the curved section.

2. Pin the curved edge of the background piece to the curved edge of the saucer center, matching the center creases and side edges. Sew together with the background piece on top. Press the seam allowance toward the background fabric.

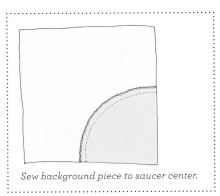

Sew background piece to saucer center.

3. Repeat Steps 1 and 2 with the same fabrics to complete 4 square sections of the saucer block.

4. Sew 2 square sections together, matching the outer edges of the saucer centers, to make a half-block. Press the seam allowance to the left.

Note: If you are using a directional print, pay attention to the orientation of the print as you assemble the block.

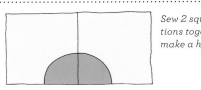

Sew 2 square sections together to make a half-block.

5. Sew the remaining 2 square sections in the block together, again matching the outer edges of the saucer centers. Press the seam allowances to the right.

6. Sew the 2 half-blocks together so that the saucer centers make a circle to complete the saucer block. Press the seams open.

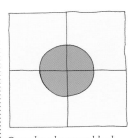

Completed saucer block

7. Repeat Steps 1–6 to make all of the blocks required for the quilt.

Assemble

1. Sew 4 saucer blocks together, working from left to right, to make a row. Repeat this step to make 5 rows.

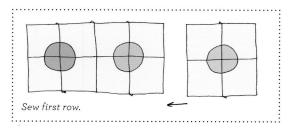

Sew first row.

2. Press the vertical seam allowances of each row in alternating directions.

3. Working from top to bottom, sew the rows together. Nest seam allowances and align seams.

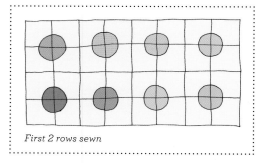

First 2 rows sewn

4. Press the row seams down toward the lower edge of the quilt.

Finish

Refer to Quilting Tips (pages 26–32) for quilting and finishing.

1. Layer the quilt top, batting, and backing.

2. Baste the quilt to prepare for quilting.

3. Free-motion machine quilt using a loopy, allover design.

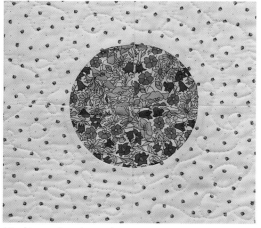

Machine quilt in loopy design.

4. Square up if needed and bind the quilt.

TWIN SIZE (70″ × 90″)

Materials and Cutting

For 63 saucer blocks:

Fabric	Yardage	Cutting
Saucer centers	21 different fabrics, each 8″ × 24″ or ⅛ yard	Cut 12 of template pattern 4A from each of the 21 fabrics.
Background prints	2⅝ yards each of 2 different fabrics	Cut 126 of template pattern 5A from each of the fabrics.
Backing	5⅝ yards	
Binding	⅝ yard	Cut 9 strips 2¼″ × width of fabric.
Batting	74″ × 94″	

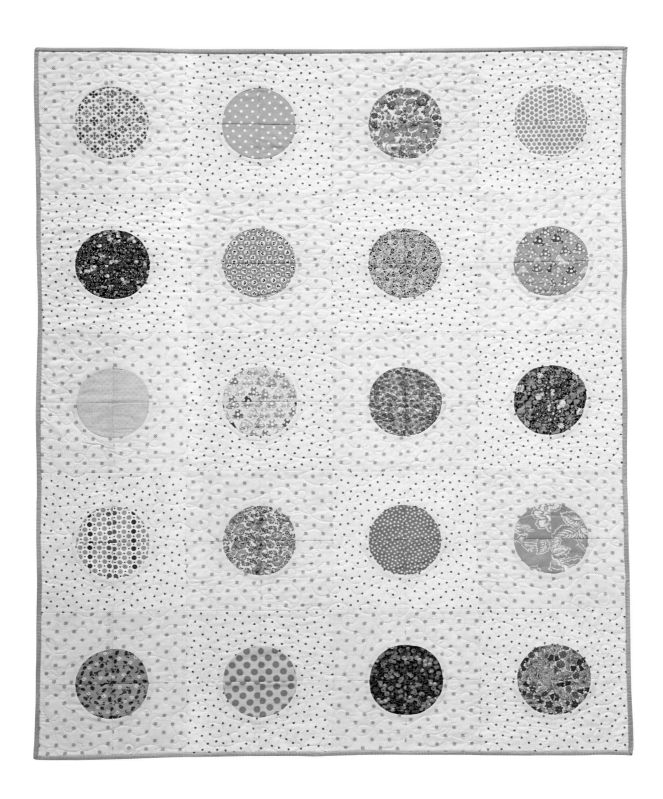

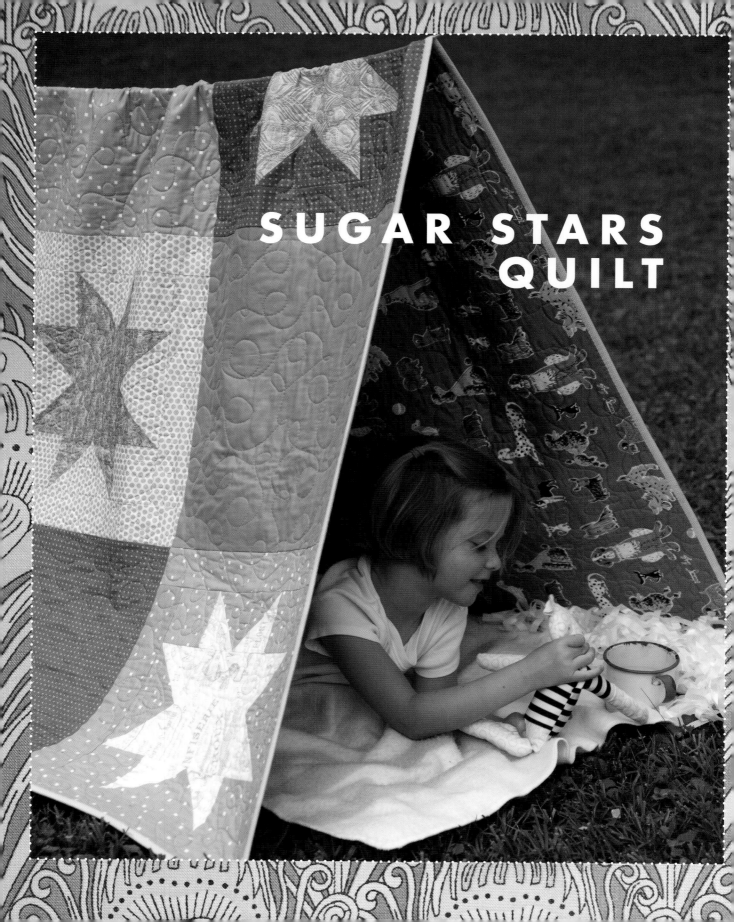

SUGAR STARS QUILT

FINISHED BLOCK SIZE: 16˝ × 16˝

FINISHED SIZE: 80˝ × 80˝ FULL

With its sparkling pink stars, this sweet quilt was inspired by two different vintage quilts. For a soft and sweet look, I paired pink and gray prints and solids.

Each star features a different Liberty of London or cotton print. Because half the blocks are simply a square of fabric, this quilt takes less time than you would think to piece. To keep the focus on those twinkling stars, I free-motion quilted in a subtle, swirling, overall design.

Supplies Needed

The fabrics shown here, paired with the Liberty Tana Lawn prints, are all woven, quilting weight, and 100% cotton.

13 different pieces 8˝ × 16˝ of pink Liberty Tana Lawn and/or cotton fabrics for the stars

1¼ yards each of 6 different gray cotton fabrics (prints and/or solids) for star backgrounds and setting squares

5 yards* backing fabric

⅝ yard binding fabric

Batting: 84˝ × 84˝

* Requires minimum 44˝ usable width of fabric. If your fabric is narrower, you will need additional yardage to piece the backing.

Cutting

Pink Tana Lawn and Cotton Prints

From each of the 13 fabrics:
Cut 1 square 6½˝ × 6½˝ for star center.

Cut 4 squares 3⅞˝ × 3⅞˝; cut in half diagonally for star point triangles.

Gray Background Fabrics
From each of the 6 fabrics:
Cut 2 squares 16½˝ × 16½˝ for setting squares.

Cut 2 squares 7¼˝ × 7¼˝; cut in half diagonally. Cut in half

diagonally again for the star point background triangles.

Cut 8 squares 3½˝ × 3½˝ for Star block corner squares.

Cut 4 rectangles 2½˝ × 12½˝ for Star block horizontal sashing.

Cut 4 rectangles 2½˝ × 16½˝ for Star block vertical sashing.

Binding Fabric
Cut 9 strips 2¼˝ × width of fabric.

CONSTRUCTION

Unless otherwise indicated, use a ¼˝ seam allowance and sew all seams with the right sides of the fabric facing each other.

Prepare

Organize your blocks for sewing by making individual stacks for each Star block. Each stack should contain 1 star center and 8 star point triangles all from the same star fabric, and 4 corner squares, 4 star point background triangles, and 2 vertical and 2 horizontal sashing pieces all from the same background print fabric.

Sew

STAR BLOCKS

Begin with a Star block stack.

1. To make the star point units, sew the long side of one star point triangle to a short side of a star point background triangle. Press the seam allowance toward the darker fabric.

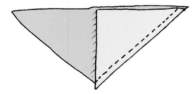

2. Sew the long side of a second star point triangle to the remaining shorter side of the unit from Step 1. Press the seam allowance toward the darker fabric to complete the star point unit.

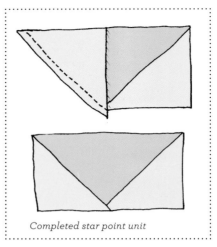

Completed star point unit

3. Repeat Steps 1 and 2 to make a total of 4 star point units.

4. Sew a corner square to each short side of a star point unit to make a star point row. Press the seam allowances outward. Repeat this step to make a second star point row.

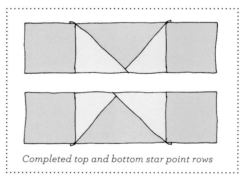

Completed top and bottom star point rows

5. Sew a remaining star point unit to 2 opposite sides of the center square. Press the seam allowances toward the center square.

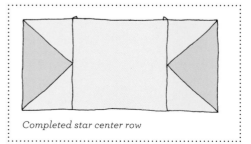

Completed star center row

6. Sew the 3 rows together to complete the block. Nest the seam allowances and make sure to align seams. Press.

7. Sew 2½˝ × 12½˝ horizontal sashing strips to top and bottom of the Star block. Press. Sew 2½˝ × 16½˝ vertical sashing strips to the sides of the Star block. Press.

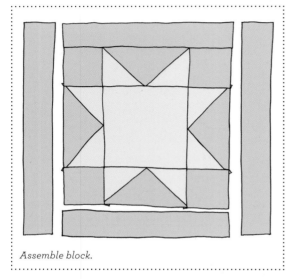

Assemble block.

8. Repeat Steps 1–7 to complete 13 Star blocks for the quilt.

Assemble

1. Referring to the finished quilt photo (page 55) for placement, lay out the Star blocks and setting squares in rows of 5.

2. For each row, beginning at the top, work from left to right to sew the blocks together to complete the row. Repeat to make a total of 5 rows.

3. Press the vertical seam allowances of rows in alternating directions.

4. Working from top to bottom, sew the rows together. Nest the seam allowances and make sure to align seams.

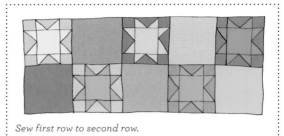

Sew first row to second row.

5. Press the row seam allowances down toward the lower edge of the quilt.

Finish

Refer to Quilting Tips (pages 26–32) for quilting and finishing.

1. Layer the quilt top, batting, and backing.

2. Baste the quilt to prepare for quilting.

3. Machine quilt in a swirling, free-motion, allover design.

Machine quilt in a swirling design.

4. Square up if needed and bind the quilt.

A
PARADE
OF
QUILTS

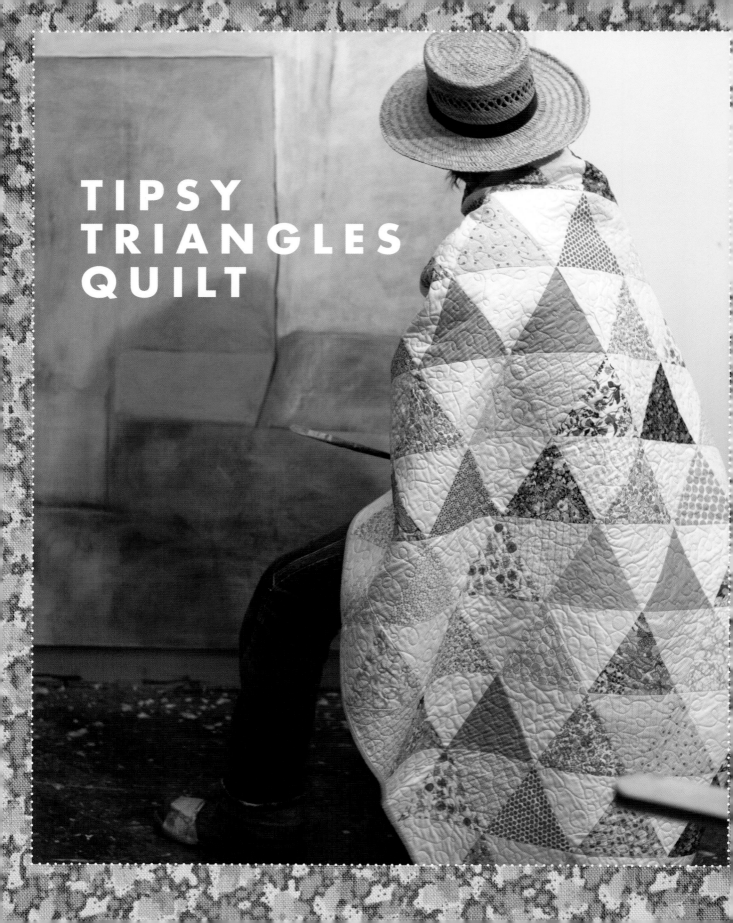

TIPSY TRIANGLES QUILT

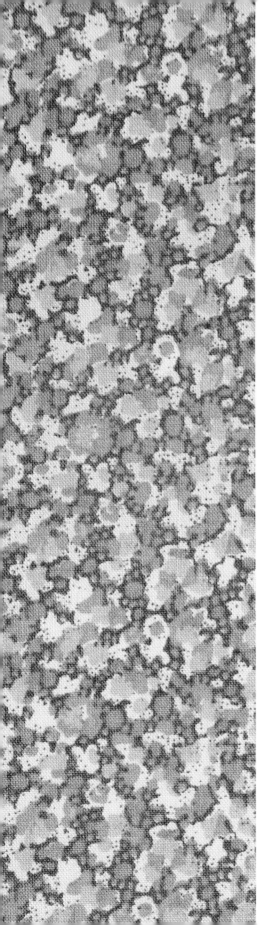

TIPSY TRIANGLES QUILT

FINISHED SIZE
59 3/8″ × 65″ THROW

This one-block quilt was inspired by the warm afternoon glow of sunshine in my parents' back garden. Its rows of alternating cream and colored print triangles are easy to piece.

This scrappy quilt combines warm-hued Liberty of London and vintage reproduction fabrics with a variety of tonal cream solids and subtle prints for a very washed-out, antique look. I chose to machine quilt in a loopy free-motion design. The curves in the quilting play against the angles and strong diagonal lines in the piecing.

Supplies Needed

The fabrics shown here, paired with the Liberty Tana Lawn prints, are all woven, quilting weight, and 100% cotton.

¼ yard each of 20 different Liberty Tana Lawn and cotton prints in various colors for triangles

⅜ yard each of 8 different cream-toned solid or print fabrics

4 yards backing fabric

½ yard binding fabric

Batting: 63″ × 69″

Cutting

Template patterns are on tissue paper pattern sheets.

Colored Tana Lawn and Cotton Prints

Cut 108 of template 6A for triangles.

Cut 6 and 6 reversed of template 7A for setting triangles.

Cream-Toned Solid and Print Fabrics

Cut 108 of template 6A for background triangles.

Cut 6 and 6 reversed of template 7A for background setting triangles.

Binding Fabric

Cut 7 strips 2¼″ × width of fabric.

CONSTRUCTION

Unless otherwise indicated, use a ¼˝ seam allowance and sew all seams with the right sides of the fabric facing each other.

Sew

ROW A

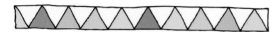

1. To assemble row A, begin with a colored print setting triangle (7A) and a background triangle (6A). Sew the long side of the print setting triangle to the left side of the background triangle.

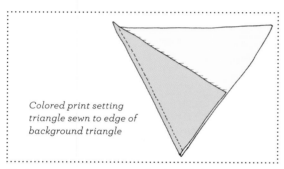

Colored print setting triangle sewn to edge of background triangle

2. Continue sewing triangles from left to right, alternating colored print triangles pointing up and background triangles pointing down, until you have pieced 9 colored print triangles in the row (not counting the setting triangle). End with a background setting triangle (7A). Press seams to the right as you go.

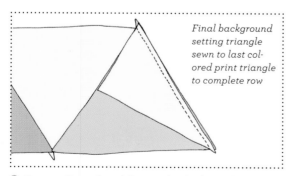

Final background setting triangle sewn to last colored print triangle to complete row

3. Repeat Steps 1 and 2 to make 6 of row A.

ROW B

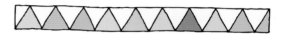

1. Assemble row B in the same fashion as row A, but begin with a reversed background setting triangle (7AR) and a colored print triangle (6A), pointing up, instead. Piece triangles until you have 9 background triangles (not counting the setting triangle) in the row. End with a reversed print setting triangle (7AR).

2. Repeat Step 1 to complete 6 of row B.

Assemble

Working from top to bottom, sew the rows together, matching triangle points to align seams. Press seam allowances down toward the lower edge of the quilt.

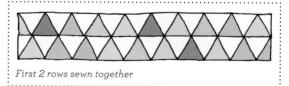

First 2 rows sewn together

Finish

Refer to Quilting Tips (pages 26–32) for quilting and finishing.

1. Layer the quilt top, batting, and backing.

2. Baste the quilt to prepare for quilting.

3. Free-motion machine quilt using a loopy, allover design.

4. Square up if needed and bind the quilt.

T I P *If you want to quilt in a different style, go for it!
I encourage you to get creative. This quilt would look
beautiful with geometric, straight-line quilting.*

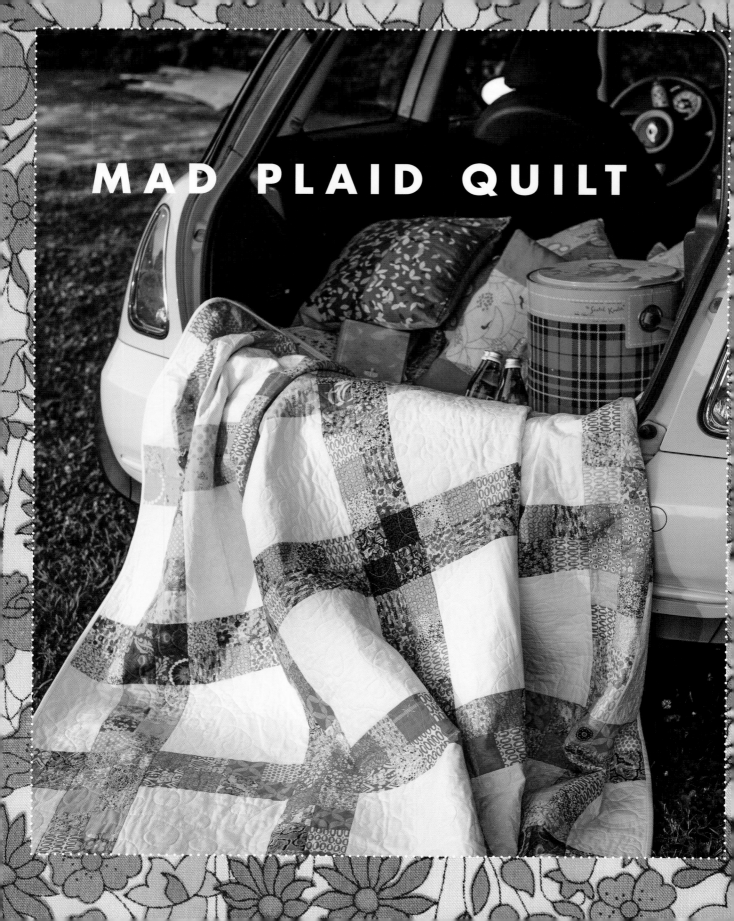

MAD PLAID QUILT

MAD PLAID QUILT

FINISHED SIZE: 90˝ × 90˝ QUEEN

This quilt is inspired by the transparency and blending of color in woven plaid fabric. With its summery, bright colors, the Mad Plaid is cheery and makes me want to grab a book and a glass of lemonade.

Each color used in the quilt overlaps four other colors. When two of the colors intersect and overlap in the design, the color of the block changes as if the two overlapping colors were blended together. The fabric color selection is the key to this pattern, so choose fabrics carefully.

For the colored "plaid" stripes I used a variety of vivid Liberty of London Tana Lawn and cotton prints. Many of the prints have a summery 1960s feel to coordinate with the Poppy and Daisy Liberty print fabric used on the back of the quilt. To give the background some interest, the squares are made up of a variety of white-on-white prints.

Because I was looking for something that would allow the overall plaid effect of the design to be the focus of the quilt, I decided on a loopy free-motion quilting design.

Supplies Needed

The fabrics shown here, paired with the Liberty Tana Lawn prints, are all woven, quilting weight, and 100% cotton.

1 strip 3˝ × width of fabric of 8 different Liberty Tana Lawn or cotton prints for "plaid" Four-Patches in each of the following colors: aqua, yellow, blue, and green (32 strips total)

2 strips 3˝ × width of fabric of 8 different Liberty Tana Lawn or cotton prints for "plaid" Four-Patches in shades of pink (16 strips total)

1 strip 3˝ × 26˝ of 2 different Liberty Tana Lawn or cotton prints for overlapping "plaid" Four-Patches in each of the following colors: lilac, purple, orange, intense pink, yellow green, pink-and-green print, and blue green (14 strips total)

1 strip 3˝ × 20˝ of 2 different Liberty Tana Lawn or cotton prints for overlapping "plaid" Four-Patches in each of the following colors: intense aqua and intense green (4 strips total)

Supplies Needed, continued

1 piece 3˝ × 8˝ of 2 different Liberty Tana Lawn or cotton prints for overlapping "plaid" Four-Patches in each of the following colors: intense blue and intense yellow (4 strips total)

¾ yard each of 5 different white-on-white print fabrics for background

8 yards backing fabric or 5½ yards if using Liberty fabric

¾ yard binding fabric

Batting: 94˝ × 94˝

Cutting

White-on-White Prints

From each fabric:
Cut 5 squares 10½˝ × 10½˝ for inner background.

Cut 4 rectangles 5½˝ × 10½˝ for outer background.

From 4 of the fabrics:
Cut 1 square 5½˝ × 5½˝ for background corners.

Binding Fabric
Cut 10 strips 2¼˝ × width of fabric.

CONSTRUCTION

Unless otherwise indicated, use a ¼˝ seam allowance and sew all seams with the right sides of the fabric facing each other.

Sew

STRIP PIECE FOUR-PATCH UNITS

> **T I P** *When strip-piecing the Four-Patch units, I like to decrease my machine's stitch length to 1.5 so that the strip seams do not come apart as I handle the subcut pieces.*

1. Begin with the 8 aqua strips 3˝ × width of fabric. Make pairs of strips. Sew each pair together along a long side. Press.

Pair of aqua strips sewn together

2. Subcut each set of sewn strips into 12 pieced rectangles 3˝ × 5½˝.

3. Sew together a pair of pieced rectangles, both cut from the same strip set, reversing the fabric orientation to create a Four-Patch unit with matching fabrics on the diagonal from each other. Press.

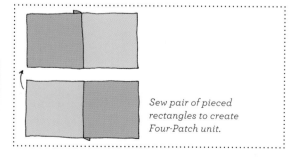

Sew pair of pieced rectangles to create Four-Patch unit.

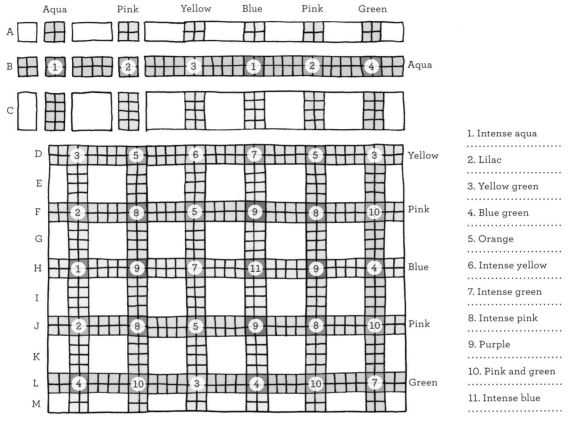

Quilt assembly diagram

4. Repeat Steps 1–3 with the remaining cut sections until you have 24 aqua Four-Patch units, 6 from each strip set.

5. Repeat Steps 1–4 to make 24 Four-Patch units from each of the following colors: yellow, blue, and green.

6. Repeat Steps 1–4 with the pink strips to make 48 pink Four-Patch units.

7. Repeat Steps 1–4 to make the following Four-Patches:

4 Four-Patches each of lilac, purple, orange, intense pink, yellow green, pink-and-green print, and blue green

3 Four-Patches each of intense aqua and intense green

1 Four-Patch each of intense blue and intense yellow

SEW ROWS

Follow the quilt assembly diagram for block placement (page 65).

1. Sew together 2 aqua Four-Patch units from different strip sets to create a vertical unit. Press.

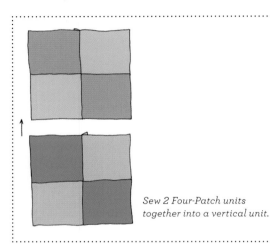

Sew 2 Four-Patch units together into a vertical unit.

2. Repeat Step 1 to make the following vertical units: 5 each aqua, yellow, blue, and green; and 10 pink. Set aside until you make Rows C, E, G, I, and K.

3. To make row A, referring to the quilt assembly diagram for color placement, sew the 5½˝ × 5½˝ background corner squares, Four-Patch units, and 5½˝ × 10½˝ outer background rectangles together from left to right. Press all seam allowances to the same side. Repeat this step to make row M.

4. To make Rows C, E, G, I, and K, repeat Step 3 with the 5½˝ × 10½˝ outer background rectangles, the vertical units from Step 2, and the 10½˝ × 10½˝ inner background squares, sewing in the order shown in the quilt assembly diagram. Press seam allowances in same direction as rows A and M.

5. To make rows B, D, F, H, J, and L, sew together 18 of the Four-Patch units that correspond to the colors in the quilt assembly diagram for each row. Press seam allowances in the opposite direction as you did in Step 4.

Assemble

1. Working from top to bottom, sew the rows together. Nest seam allowances and align seams.

2. Press the row seams down toward the lower edge of the quilt.

Finish

Refer to Quilting Tips (pages 26–32) for quilting and finishing.

1. Layer the quilt top, batting, and backing.

2. Baste the quilt to prepare for quilting.

3. Machine quilt in a loopy, free-motion, allover design.

4. Square up if needed and bind the quilt.

CLASSIC THREAD
SPOOL QUILTS

FINISHED BLOCK SIZE: 14˝ × 14˝

FINISHED SIZE: 82˝ × 82˝ QUEEN

FINISHED MINI-QUILT SIZE: 17˝ × 17˝

Note: See mini-quilt instructions (page 74).

I first became obsessed with Thread Spool quilt blocks a few years ago when I saw a gorgeous vintage Thread Spool quilt online. Creating a queen-size quilt with a plethora of Liberty of London prints as the centers of the spools has been stuck in my mind ever since. I am so happy with the final result of that long-contemplated inspiration.

I paired 50 different Liberty of London and quilting cotton prints for the spool centers, with some of my favorite text, sewing-themed, and map-print fabrics for the spool ends. All of the spools are then bordered and sashed using a variety of white-on-white prints.

To echo the image of crossing threads, I machine-quilted this quilt in a loopy allover design with zigzag quilting in each spool center.

Supplies Needed

All of the fabrics shown here, paired with the Liberty Tana Lawn prints, are woven, quilting weight, and 100% cotton. To achieve the wide variety of Liberty prints in this quilt, I used a Liberty color wheel bundle from Purl Soho.

50 different pieces 5˝ × 9˝ of Liberty Tana Lawn or cotton prints in a variety of colors for spool centers

½ yard each of 5 different prints for spool ends

1⅓ yards each of 5 different white-on-white fabrics for block backgrounds and sashing

5 yards* backing fabric

⅝ yard binding fabric

Batting: 86˝ × 86˝

* Requires minimum 44˝ usable width of fabric. If your fabric is narrower, you will need additional yardage to piece the backing.

Cutting

Tana Lawn or Cotton Print Spool Center Fabrics

Cut 100 squares 4¼˝ × 4¼˝ (2 from each of 50 fabrics).

Spool End Fabrics

From each of the 5 different fabrics:

Cut 40 squares 2⅛˝ × 2⅛˝ for spool half-square triangle units.

Cut 40 rectangles 1¾˝ × 4¼˝ for spool ends.

Binding Fabric

Cut 9 strips 2¼˝ × width of fabric.

White-on-White Print Fabrics

From the 5 different fabrics, cut a total of:

200 squares 2⅛˝ × 2⅛˝ for spool half-square triangle units

200 rectangles 1¾˝ × 4¼˝ for spool side backgrounds

50 rectangles 2˝ × 6¾˝ for spool sashing

25 rectangles 2˝ × 14½˝ for spool sashing

30 rectangles 2½˝ × 14½˝ for block sashing

15 strips 2½˝ × width of fabric for sashing rows

CONSTRUCTION

Unless otherwise indicated, use a ¼˝ seam allowance and sew all seams with the right sides of the fabric facing each other.

Sew

SPOOL BLOCKS

Each Spool block is made up of 4 individual spool units.

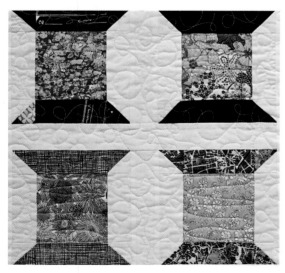

Completed Spool block

Half-Square Triangle Units

1. Mark a diagonal line on the wrong side of each white 2⅛˝ × 2⅛˝ square.

2. Pair up each white square with a print square, right sides together. Sew 2 seams offset ¼˝ from the marked line in each pair of squares.

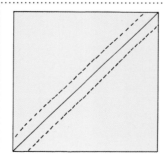

Sew 2 seams in each pair of squares.

3. Cut each pair along the marked line and press the seam allowances open. Each pair makes 2 half-square triangle units. Keep pairs together for ease of assembly later.

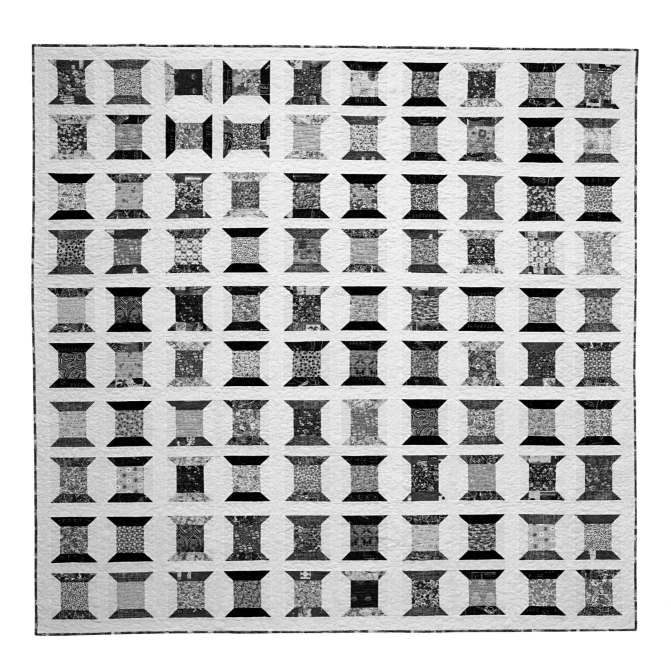

Spool Ends

1. Sew a matching fabric half-square triangle unit to each short end of a 1¾˝ × 4¼˝ spool end rectangle as shown. Press the seam allowances away from the center rectangle.

Completed spool end, with matching fabrics. Make 200.

2. Repeat Step 1 to make a total of 200 spool end units.

Spool Centers

1. Sew a white 1¾˝ × 4¼˝ background rectangle to a 4¼˝ × 4¼˝ spool center square. Sew another white background rectangle to the opposite side of the square. Press the seam allowances toward the spool center. Mixing up the white-on-white prints here gives the quilt depth and variety, but you can match them if you prefer.

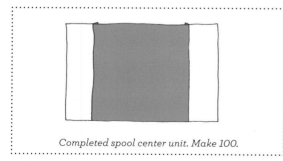

Completed spool center unit. Make 100.

2. Repeat Step 1 to make a total of 100 spool center units.

Assemble Spool

1. Sew matching spool ends to the upper and lower edges of a spool center. Nest seam allowances to align seams.

2. Repeat Step 1 to make 100 spool units. Press.

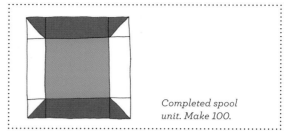

Completed spool unit. Make 100.

Assemble Block

1. Sew a white 2˝ × 6¾˝ spool sashing rectangle to the right side of a completed spool unit.

2. Sew a second spool unit to the opposite side of the spool sashing. Press the seam allowances toward the sashing.

3. Repeat Steps 1 and 2 to make 50 units of 2 spools each.

4. Sew a 2˝ × 14½˝ spool sashing rectangle to the lower edge of a 2-spool unit, matching the long edges. Make sure you're not using the wider block sashing strips.

5. Sew another 2-spool unit to the lower edge of the spool sashing. Press the seam allowances toward the sashing.

6. Repeat Steps 1–5 to complete each of the 25 blocks required for the quilt.

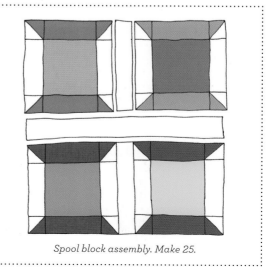

Spool block assembly. Make 25.

Assemble

Note: I have turned just one block on its side in my quilt, but you could turn more blocks if you like!

1. Begin with the first row of the quilt. Sew 5 Spool blocks together with 2½″ × 14½″ block sashing strips between the blocks, beginning and ending the row with a block sashing strip. Press the seam allowances toward the sashing.

2. Repeat Step 1 to make a total of 5 rows.

3. Sew the 15 white 2½″ × width of fabric strips together at the short ends to make a continuous piece. Press.

4. Measure your pressed block rows to check the width, which ideally is 82½″. Cut 7 sashing row strips to this measurement from the continuous strip made in Step 3. Note: If the rows are much

wider than 82½″, you may need to cut and add another width-of-fabric strip to the continuous strip.

5. Sew the block rows together, with sashing rows between each pair, beginning and ending the quilt with a sashing row. Press the seam allowances toward the sashing.

Finish

Refer to Quilting Tips (pages 26–32) for quilting and finishing.

1. Layer the quilt top, batting, and backing.

2. Baste the quilt to prepare for quilting.

3. Machine quilt in a loopy free-motion allover design with zigzag free-motion in the spool centers.

4. Square up if needed and bind the quilt.

Completed free-motion quilting in allover loopy/zigzag design

Supplies Needed

1 piece 5˝ × 5˝ of 4 different Liberty of London Tana Lawn or cotton prints in a variety of colors for spool centers

1 piece 5˝ × 9˝ of 4 different prints for spool ends

1 fat quarter white-on-white print fabric for block background

1 fat quarter border fabric

⅝ yard backing fabric

¼ yard binding fabric

Batting: 21˝ × 21˝

Cutting

Tana Lawn or Cotton Print Spool Center Fabrics

Cut 4 squares 4¼˝ × 4¼˝.

Spool End Fabrics

From each of the 4 different fabrics:

Cut 2 squares 2⅛˝ × 2⅛˝ for spool half-square triangle units.

Cut 2 rectangles 1¾˝ × 4¼˝ for spool ends.

White-on-White Print Fabrics

Cut 8 squares 2⅛˝ × 2⅛˝ for spool half-square triangle units.

Cut 8 rectangles 1¾˝ × 4¼˝ for spool side backgrounds.

Cut 2 rectangles 2˝ × 6¾˝ for spool setting strips.

Cut 1 rectangle 2˝ × 14½˝ for spool setting strips.

Border Fabric

Cut 2 rectangles 2˝ × 14½˝ for border.

Cut 2 rectangles 2˝ × 17½˝ for border.

Binding Fabric

Cut 2 strips 2¼˝ × width of fabric.

Sew

1. Follow *Thread Spool Quilt* instructions (pages 70–72) to assemble the Thread Spool block.

2. Sew the 2 shorter border strips to the top and bottom of the completed Thread Spool block. Press the seam allowances toward the border (Figure A).

3. Sew the 2 longer border strips to the left and right sides of the block. Press the seam allowances toward the border.

4. Follow the *Thread Spool Quilt* instructions for finishing (page 73).

Figure A. Sew borders to block.

Thread Spool *mini-quilt*

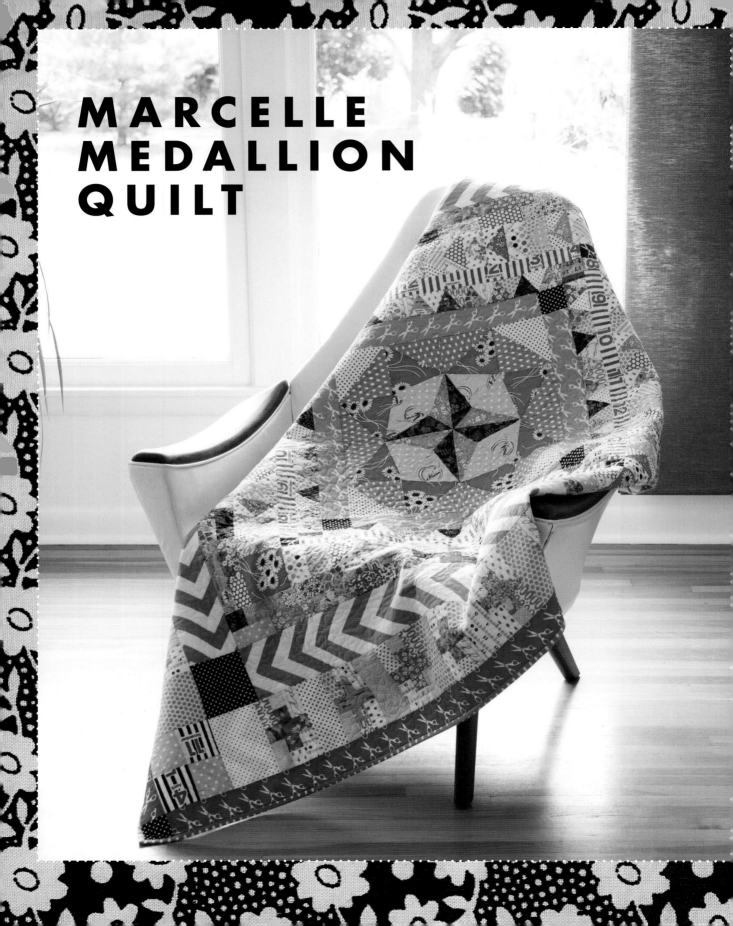

MARCELLE
MEDALLION
QUILT

FINISHED SIZE: 59˝ × 59˝ THROW

This throw-sized medallion quilt is not for the faint of heart. I designed this namesake quilt with lovers of piecing in mind. With a center Star block inspired by a vintage quilt and ten rows of borders, this quilt involves a lot of piecing. I think of this as a quilt to bite off in small chunks, working on just one border at a time, watching the quilt grow. Although there is a lot of it, the piecing is actually very straightforward. The center block is the only section with more difficult seams. If you're a lover of piecing or a quilter looking for a challenge, I hope you will love making this quilt. You may even find yourself experimenting with additional borders of your own design!

For this quilt I paired tons of Liberty of London Tana Lawn scraps with bright, colorful prints (including some of my favorite scissor prints from Moda and text prints by Suzuko Koseki), gray accents, and dotty white background prints. This quilt is busy and intense, and shows off the work involved. To let the piecing be the star, I free-motion quilted in an allover stipple design.

Supplies Needed

The fabrics shown here, paired with the Liberty of London Tana Lawn prints, are all woven, quilting weight, and 100% cotton.

4 yards backing fabric

½ yard binding fabric

Batting: 63˝ × 63˝

Fabric and Cutting Lists by Border

If you want to choose each border fabric separately, use the fabric requirements listed by border row on the next three pages. If you want a scrappy look, as shown, the total yardage required of Liberty of London Tana Lawn or colorful cotton print fabric is 4 yards; you also will need 3 yards total of light background and gray background prints.

Note: Because of the number of pieces in each border row, it is easy for small inaccuracies to add up. This can make the borders too short or too long. To ensure the solid borders are the right size, I suggest you measure the quilt top as you add each pieced row to the center medallion block, and then cut the solid borders based on your actual measurements.

Template patterns are on tissue paper pattern sheets.

CENTER BLOCK

½ yard total of at least 5 different colors of Liberty of London Tana Lawn or cotton prints for inner and outer stars and inner star background

⅛ yard gray print for background

⅛ yard light-colored print for background

Tana Lawn and colored prints

Cut 4 each of template pieces D and E from the same color for outer star points.

Cut 4 of template piece G from another color for star background.

Cut 4 of template piece H from a third color for star points.

Cut 4 of template piece I from a fourth color for star background.

Cut 4 of template piece J from a fifth color for star points.

Gray print background

Cut 4 each of the following template pieces:

AB for outer star background

F for outer star background

C for outer star background

Light print background

Cut 4 of template piece AB for corner triangles.

BORDER 1

¼ yard print border

1 print piece at least 6˝ × 6˝ for corner squares

Tana Lawn and cotton prints

Cut 4 border strips 2½˝ × 16½˝.

Cut 4 corner squares 2½˝ × 2½˝.

BORDER 2

¼ yard total colored prints for triangles

¼ yard total background prints for triangles

1 print piece at least 5˝ × 5˝ for corner squares

Tana Lawn and cotton prints

Cut 40 of template pattern MM for triangles.

Cut 4 squares 2¼˝ × 2¼˝ for corner blocks.

Background fabric

Cut 36 of template pattern MM for triangles.

Cut 4 and 4 reversed of pattern piece MA for setting triangles.

BORDER 3

¼ yard print border

1 print piece at least 5˝ × 5˝ for corner squares

Tana Lawn and cotton prints

Cut 4 border strips 1¾˝ × 24˝.

Cut 4 corner squares 1¾˝ × 1¾˝.

BORDER 4

⅓ yard total colored prints for Flying Geese centers

⅓ yard total background prints for Flying Geese sides

1 print piece at least 10˝ × 10˝ for corner squares

Tana Lawn and cotton prints

Cut 32 squares 3⅛˝ × 3⅛˝, and then cut in half diagonally once for Flying Geese center triangles.

Cut 4 squares 3¾˝ × 3¾˝ for corner squares.

Background fabric

Cut 32 squares 3½˝ × 3½˝, and then cut in half diagonally twice for Flying Geese side triangles.

BORDER 5

½ yard total colored prints for bricks

Tana Lawn and cotton prints

Cut 92 rectangles 1¾˝ × 3¾˝ for bricks.

BORDER 6

½ yard print border

1 print piece at least 10˝ × 10˝ for corner squares

Tana Lawn and cotton prints

Cut 4 border strips 4¼˝ × 38˝.

Cut 4 corner squares 4¼˝ × 4¼˝.

BORDER 7

½ yard total colored prints for crosses (at least a 4″ × 4″ piece of fabric is required to make a Cross block of a single print)

....

1⅛ yards total light-colored prints for cross background

....

⅛ yard each of a light-colored and a bright-colored print for corner squares

....

Tana Lawn and cotton prints

Note: If you would like each of the crosses to be made of a single print fabric, you will need 2 cross squares and 1 cross rectangle from each print.

Cut 64 squares 1½″ × 1½″ for cross ends.

Cut 32 rectangles 1½″ × 3½″ for cross centers.

Cut 8 squares 3″ × 3″ for corner blocks (light-colored print).

Cut 8 squares 3″ × 3″ for corner blocks (bright-colored print).

Background fabric

Cut 64 squares 1½˝ × 1½˝ for cross background.

Cut 128 rectangles 1½˝ × 2½˝ for cross background.

Cut 28 sashing strips 2½˝ × 5½˝.

Cut 8 sashing strips 4˝ × 5½˝.

BORDER 8

½ yard print border

1 print piece at least 8˝ × 8˝ for corner squares

Tana Lawn and cotton prints

Cut 6 border strips 2½˝ × width of fabric. Sew the strips end to end using a ¼˝ seam allowance; then cut the strips into 4 border strips 2½˝ × 55½˝.

Cut 4 corner squares 2½˝ × 2½˝.

Binding fabric

Cut 7 strips 2¼˝ × width of fabric.

SEW

Center Star Block

PIECING QUARTER-STAR UNITS

1. On the wrong side of cut fabric pieces AB, D, E, G, and I, mark a small dot on the seamline intersections, which are indicated by a circle on each template pattern.

2. Sew each of the following sets of 2 pieces together: light AB and gray AB (to yield a 4˝ finished half-square triangle unit); C and D; E and F; G and H; and I and J. Match the edges that will be joined by matching like symbols on the template patterns.

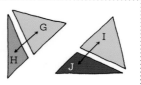

3. Sew the first set-in seam by sewing the pieced I/J unit to the pieced G/H unit, starting at what will be the outer edge of the quarter-block and stopping at the marked dot on I. Backstitch at dot. Finger-press the seam open.

4. Sew D/C to the I side of the unit from Step 3, beginning at the outer block edge, stopping at the marked dot on I, and backstitching. This line of stitching should meet the previous line exactly.

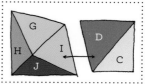

5. Repeat Step 4 to add pieced unit E/F and then pieced unit AB. The final seam will join the B side of unit AB to the D side of D/C to make a completed quarter-star unit. Press.

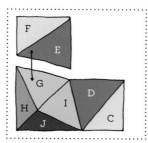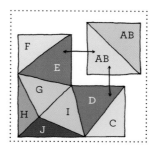

6. Repeat Steps 1–5 to make a total of 4 quarter-star units.

ASSEMBLE CENTER STAR BLOCK

1. Sew the upper 2 quarter-star units together, aligning F and H edges and matching points. Repeat this step with the lower 2 quarter-star units. Press the seam allowances open.

2. Sew the upper half-star unit to the lower half-star unit, aligning J and C edges and matching points. Press the seam allowances open.

BORDERS 1, 3, 6, AND 8

Remember to check that the cut border lengths match the completed pieced borders before assembling. Sew a corresponding corner square to each end of 2 border strips from each set of 4 border strips. Press.

BORDER 2

1. Refer to *Tipsy Triangles Quilt*, Row B (page 60) to piece 10 print triangles (MM), 9 background triangles (MM), and 1 and 1R background setting triangles (MA) as shown. Press seams to the right as you go.

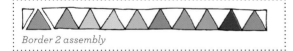

Border 2 assembly

2. Repeat Step 1 to make a total of 4 triangle borders.

3. Sew a corner square to each end of 2 triangle borders.

BORDER 4

1. Make 64 Flying Geese units as shown.

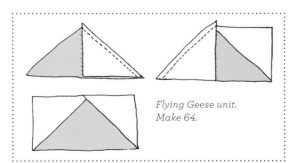

Flying Geese unit. Make 64.

2. Sew 4 Flying Geese borders of 16 Flying Geese units each. Sew a corner square to each end of 2 border strips.

BORDER 5

1. Sew 22 bricks together end to end along short ends. Press. Repeat to make a second set.

2. Sew the long sides of the 2 pieced brick strips together, offsetting the first 2 bricks by 1¼˝. Press. Cut into 2 sections, each 3˝ × 33˝.

3. Repeat Steps 1 and 2 with 2 sets of 24 bricks. Cut pieced brick strip into 2 sections, each 3˝ × 38˝.

BORDER 7

Assemble Cross Block

TIP *If you want each of the crosses to be made of one print, take the time now to organize the components of each block into piles containing the same print fabrics. Each block requires 1 center print rectangle and 2 pieced small print square/background rectangle units.*

Follow the assembly diagram to complete 32 Cross blocks. Press toward the lighter color.

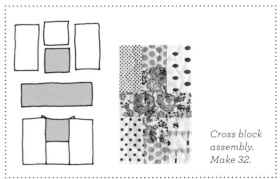

Cross block assembly. Make 32.

Assemble Corner Blocks

Follow the assembly diagram to complete 4 Four-Patch units for corner blocks. Press toward darker color.

Corner block assembly. Make 4.

Assemble Cross Block Borders

1. Sew 8 Cross blocks together with 2½˝ × 5½˝ sashing strips between. Begin and end the row with a 4½˝ × 5½˝ sashing strip. Press after each addition. Repeat this step to make a total of 4 Cross borders.

2. Sew a corner block to each end of 2 border strips.

Quilt assembly diagram

ASSEMBLE

1. Following the assembly diagram for placement, begin by sewing a Border 1, without corner squares, to the left and right sides of the center Star block.

2. Sew the Border 1s with corner squares to the top and bottom of the center medallion.

3. Continue to sew each consecutive set of borders, first to the sides and then to the top and bottom. Press seam allowances as you go.

FINISH

Refer to Quilting Tips (pages 26–32) for quilting and finishing.

1. Layer the quilt top, batting, and backing.

2. Baste the quilt to prepare for quilting.

3. Machine quilt using stipple free-motion quilting.

4. Square up if needed and bind the quilt.

A LITTLE LIBERTY

LIBERTY BLOOM

Perfect for your favorite coat or sweater, this simple no-sew flower brooch is a great afternoon project. Using just scraps, glue, felt, and some interfacing, these blooms are also inexpensive to make!

I used a variety of blossom-hued Liberty of London print scraps for the flowers and a green print for each flower leaf.

Supplies Needed

For each flower:

1 strip 2½″ × 36″ Liberty fabric	1 square 3″ × 3″ green print fabric
1 square 3″ × 3″ heavyweight interfacing	1 bar-style pin back, ¾″ long
1 square 3″ × 3″ felt	Glue (Fabri-Tac works well)

Cutting

Felt

Use the second-largest circle from the Little Dorothy's Embellished T-Shirt appliqué patterns (on tissue paper pattern sheets) to cut out a circle 1¾″ in diameter.

Heavyweight Interfacing

Use the third-largest circle from the Little Dorothy's Embellished T-Shirt appliqué patterns (on tissue paper pattern sheets) to cut out a circle 1½″ in diameter.

CONSTRUCTION

Prepare

1. Use a pea-sized dab of glue to attach a short end of the Liberty strip to the center of the interfacing.

2. Fold the 3″ × 3″ green fabric square as shown to create a leaf. Glue the last fabric fold in place.

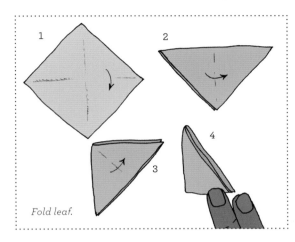

Fold leaf.

3. Let the flower and leaf dry for 1 hour.

Assemble

1. Wrap and twist the fabric strip around the glued center, placing a tiny bit of glue on the interfacing every so often to anchor the wraps in place.

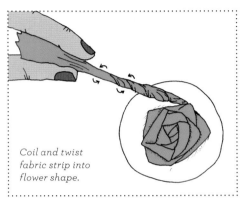

Coil and twist fabric strip into flower shape.

2. Once you have filled the entire interfacing circle, cut the strip, leaving 1″ remaining. Tuck the end around to the back of the interfacing and glue in place.

3. Glue the leaf to the back of the interfacing with the more attractive side faceup.

4. Glue the felt to the back of the interfacing and glue the pin back to the back of the felt.

Let the bloom dry for 24 hours and wear it with your favorite coat, hat, or handbag!

LOG CABIN PINCUSHION

This little pincushion is topped with a twist on the traditional Log Cabin quilt block, backed with a fun fabric, and embellished with rickrack sandwiched between the front and the back. The layer of 100% cotton batting will help keep your pins like new by cleaning them each time you place them in the pincushion. You may find this project to be one you want to make again and again for your friends who sew!

Supplies Needed

1 piece at least 1½˝ × 1½˝ of red print fabric for Log Cabin center

10 strips 1˝ wide (from 1½˝ to 6½˝ length) of a variety of blue Liberty Tana Lawn or other cotton prints for logs

10 strips 1˝ wide (from 1½˝ to 6½˝ length) of a variety of pink and red Liberty Tana Lawn or other cotton prints

¼ yard or scrap at least 7˝ × 7˝ for backing fabric (Cotton/linen, quilting-weight, or heavier bottom-weight 100% cotton all work well.)

100% cotton batting measuring at least 7˝ × 7˝ square

¾ yard ⅜˝-wide cotton rickrack

Polyester fiberfill stuffing

Cutting

Red Print

Cut 1 square ½˝ × ½˝.

Tana Lawn and Cotton Print 1˝ Strips

Arrange and cut the fabric strips according to the block diagram.

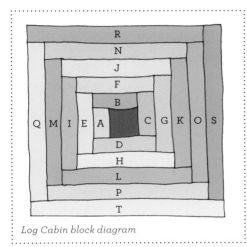

Log Cabin block diagram

From the blue fabrics, cut 1 of each of the following lengths from the 1˝-wide strips:

A: 1½˝	I: 3½˝	Q: 5½˝
B: 2˝	J: 4˝	R: 6˝
E: 2½˝	M: 4½˝	
F: 3˝	N: 5˝	

From the pink and red fabrics, cut 1 of each of the following lengths from the 1˝-wide strips:

C: 2˝	K: 4˝	S: 6˝
D: 2½˝	L: 4½˝	T: 6½˝
G: 3˝	O: 5˝	
H: 3½˝	P: 5½˝	

Backing fabric

Cut 1 square 6½˝ × 6½˝.

CONSTRUCTION

Use a generous ¼˝ seam allowance, and sew all seams with the right sides of the fabric facing each other.

Sew

CREATE THE PINCUSHION TOP

1. Sew strip A to the left side of the red print 1½˝ × 1½˝ center square. Press the seam allowance away from the center square.

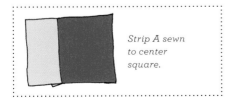

Strip A sewn to center square.

2. Sew strip B to the upper edge of the unit from Step 1. Press the seam allowance away from the center square.

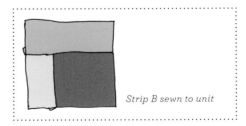

Strip B sewn to unit

3. Continue in the same fashion, sewing strips on in alphabetical order, following the block diagram above, until you have completed the Log Cabin block.

4. Layer the Log Cabin block onto the cotton batting square. Be sure that the wrong side of the Log Cabin block is touching the cotton batting layer. Press the 2 layers together.

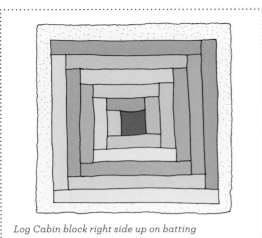

Log Cabin block right side up on batting

8. On the wrong side of the pincushion back, make 2 marks on the seam allowance about 2½˝ apart and centered on a side of the square. You will leave this section open to turn the pincushion right side out after sewing.

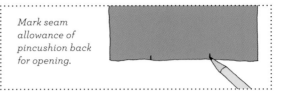

Mark seam allowance of pincushion back for opening.

Assemble

1. Pin the top and bottom (backing) of the pincushion, right sides together.

2. With the bottom of the pincushion facing up, sew the top and bottom together—begin at an opening mark, pivot at each corner, and stop when you reach the other opening mark.

3. Clip the excess seam allowance at each corner.

4. Turn the pincushion right side out.

5. Stuff the pincushion with the fiberfill until the pincushion is fairly firm.

6. Using a ladder stitch, stitch the opening of the pincushion closed.

Fill the pincushion with pins, and place it close by your machine!

5. Using a straight stitch, quilt rows of stitching every ¼˝–½˝ across the block.

6. Trim away any excess batting after quilting the pincushion top.

7. Beginning at the center of a side of the pincushion top, sew the rickrack trim in place, centering the rickrack on the ¼˝ seamline. Overlap the rickrack ends and let each veer off the seam allowance over the cut edge of the pincushion top. Backstitch a few times over the rickrack. Cut away excess.

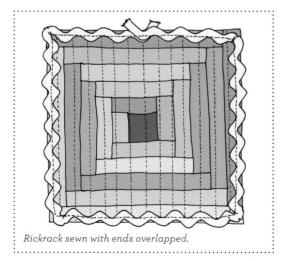

Rickrack sewn with ends overlapped.

LIBERTY HANDKERCHIEF

Supplies Needed

1 fat quarter Liberty of London Tana Lawn

1 skein 6-strand embroidery floss in a coordinating color

1 embroidery hand-sewing needle

Wash-away fabric marker for light fabrics or white transfer paper for dark fabrics

Cutting

Tana Lawn Print
    Cut 1 square 12½˝ × 12½˝.

The perfect gift for a beau, special friend, or family member, this simple, embroidered hankie sews up in a snap. With mitered corners, the hem will hold a nice point.

I used the classic Liberty of London print Betsy for the handkerchief and a coordinating red for the embroidered letter.

Pair this classic handkerchief with Walter's Tie (page 131) for a set surely destined to become a well-worn heirloom.

CONSTRUCTION

Sew

1. Press ½˝ to the wrong side all around the square of fabric.

2. Press under the raw fabric edge to the crease line pressed in Step 1.

3. Unfold the pressed edges and trim away a triangle from the outermost crease lines at each corner as shown (Figure A).

4. Press the raw edges all around back to the crease line pressed in Step 1 (Figure B).

5. Fold and press the corners toward the center of the handkerchief a scant ¼˝ at a 45° angle (Figure C).

6. Turn the edges under again at the original fold, creating a mitered hem at each corner (Figure D).

7. Topstitch along the pressed edge of the hem with a short machine stitch and pivot at each corner. Stitch around the entire handkerchief. Backstitch to finish (Figure E).

TIP *Thread a needle with a double strand of thread. Stitch through each pressed corner of the handkerchief from the right to the wrong side, going down through one side of the mitered fold and coming up just on the other side, leaving long thread tails. These threads will help you feed each corner through the machine as you sew the final stitching to hem the handkerchief. When you pivot at each corner while sewing the hem, use the threads to gently pull the corner as you begin sewing in a new direction after pivoting. This will keep the corner of the handkerchief from getting pulled down into the throat plate of the machine.*

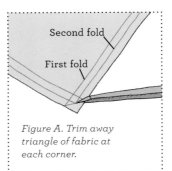

Figure A. Trim away triangle of fabric at each corner.

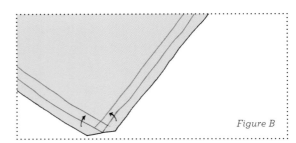

Figure B

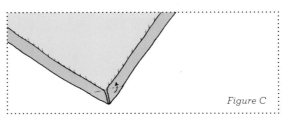

Figure C

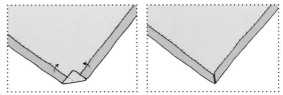

Figure D. Press corners at 45° angle, toward center of handkerchief.

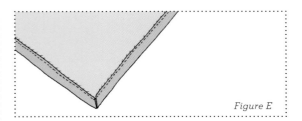

Figure E

8. Using the letter of your choice (on tissue paper pattern sheets), transfer the letter by placing the fabric over the letter and tracing with a wash-away marker. If your fabric is dark, you may need to use transfer paper and a dull pencil.

9. Embroider the letter using the stem stitch.

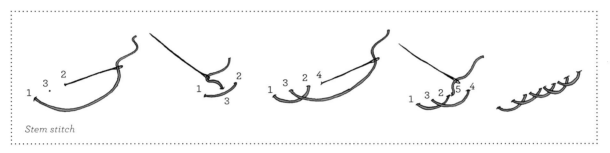

Stem stitch

Fold the handkerchief into quarters. Press. The handkerchief is now ready for gifting to your recipient or placing in your own pocket!

OLIVE'S COLLAR

Because even the family dog deserves to sport a little Liberty, I have designed a classic dog collar for the special pup in your family. It is very simple to sew, and you can find the hardware easily online if your local shop doesn't stock supplies for making collars.

I used the classic Liberty of London print Strawberry Thief for this collar. Any Liberty print, classic or seasonal, would be beautiful.

Supplies Needed

Note: If you have a hard time finding the closures, D-rings, and sliders to use, you may want to purchase a ready-made collar and reuse the findings.

⅛ yard Liberty Tana Lawn

⅛ yard midweight fusible interfacing, 45″ wide or 20″ wide for small or x-small (I use Pellon Décor Bond.)

FINISHED SIZES AND REQUIREMENTS

X-small (⅝″ × 6″–9″)

1 side release buckle ⅝″

1 slider (also called a slip-lock buckle) ⅝″

1 D-ring ⅝″

Small (¾″ × 8″–12″)

1 side release buckle ¾″

1 slider ¾″

1 D-ring ¾″

Medium (1″ × 10″–16″) or Large (1″ × 16″–26″)

1 side release buckle 1″

1 slider 1″

1 D-ring 1″

Cutting

X-Small (⅝˝ × 6˝–9˝)

Tana Lawn Print
Cut 1 rectangle 2¼˝ × 14˝.

Midweight Fusible Interfacing
Cut 1 rectangle 2¼˝ × 14˝.

Small (¾˝ × 8˝–12˝)

Tana Lawn Print
Cut 1 rectangle 3⅛˝ × 17˝.

Midweight Fusible Interfacing
Cut 1 rectangle 3⅛˝ × 17˝.

Medium (1˝ × 10˝–16˝)

Tana Lawn Print
Cut 1 rectangle 3¾˝ × 21˝.

Midweight Fusible Interfacing
Cut 1 rectangle 3¾˝ × 21˝.

Large (1˝ × 16˝–26˝)

Tana Lawn Print
Cut 1 rectangle 3¾˝ × 31˝.

Midweight Fusible Interfacing
Cut 1 rectangle 3¾˝ × 31˝.

CONSTRUCTION

- *Top stitching, unless otherwise indicated, should be spaced ⅛˝ away from edges or seams.*

- *Fuse midweight fusible interfacing to the wrong side of the corresponding Tana Lawn fabric piece, following the manufacturer's instructions.*

Sew

1. Press the collar in half lengthwise, making a crease. Fold the long cut edges in to the center crease. Press.

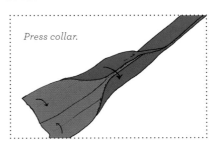

Press collar.

2. Fold the collar in half lengthwise, wrong sides together, on the pressed crease so that the raw edges are enclosed.

3. Topstitch collar along the open long side a scant ⅛˝ away from the edge. Topstitch the remaining, folded edge. Note: When you have completed the top stitching, take a look at each side of the collar and decide which will be the right side and which will be the wrong side. I find that my top stitching always looks better on the side I had faceup while sewing.

4. Fold and press an end of the collar 2˝ toward the wrong side. Fold and press this end under ¼˝ again.

5. Wrap the pressed end around the center post of the slider, with the 2˝ pressed fold at the center of the slider, and fold the wrong sides of the collar together.

6. With the ¼˝ pressed edge facing the wrong side of the collar, topstitch along the pressed edge, through both the folded end and the collar. Backstitch to reinforce.

Topstitch folded end to collar, with collar wrapped around slider post.

7. Slide the pronged end of the side release buckle onto the remaining raw end of the collar until it is approximately 2˝–3˝ away from the slider. The prongs should be pointing toward the slider.

Note: If the clip is contoured and has a right and wrong side, be sure to align with the right side of the collar.

Slide buckle onto collar.

8. Slide the remaining raw end of the collar back through the slider, the D-ring, and the opening in the other, loose end of the side release buckle.

Thread through slider, D-ring, and remaining end of side release buckle.

9. Fold and press the remaining raw end of the collar 2½˝ toward the wrong side of the collar. Press under again ¼˝ at the raw edge. Slide the clip so that it rests in the 2½˝ crease line. Slide the D-ring close to the clip.

10. Topstitch the free collar end to the collar with wrong sides together, close to the turned-under edge. Topstitch through both layers 1˝ from the side release buckle.

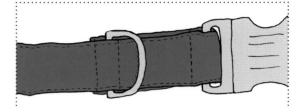

Topstitch collar with side release buckle in pressed crease and D-ring in place.

11. Slide the D-ring to the stitching line created in Step 10. With the flat part of the D-ring trapped between the second layer and the collar, topstitch as close as you can to the D-ring, through both layers, and backstitch to reinforce.

Adjust the collar using the slider, and your dog will be set to walk in style.

ACCESSORIES
FOR ALL

HIS-AND-
HER
DEVICE
CASES

HIS-AND-HER DEVICE CASES

FINISHED SIZE: BAG 10½˝ WIDE × 8½˝ TALL,
POCKET 7˝, FLAP 7½˝

These simple yet sturdy his-and-her cases will keep your device protected in style. Both his and hers have Japanese cotton/linen prints on the outside and the classic Liberty of London print Wiltshire on the interior. For his, I paired a black cotton/linen print with a deep green–hued lining. For hers, I paired a raspberry cotton/linen print with a bright raspberry–hued lining.

Supplies Needed

Makes 1 Case

⅜ yard midweight cotton/linen canvas for outer csse (A quilting-weight cotton would also work well for the exterior; I would use a lightweight fusible interfacing on the wrong side to add stability and durability.)

⅜ yard Liberty Tana Lawn for lining

Note: For napped fabrics or those with a one-way design, you will need ¾ yard for exterior and ¾ yard for lining. On the back of the case, the print will be upside down.

½ yard heavyweight double-sided fusible interfacing, 20˝ wide (I use fast2fuse.)

⅜ yard lightweight fusible poly-ester batting, 44˝ wide (I use Pellon Fusible Fleece.)

2 colored, metal-free hair elastics to coordinate with the outer bag fabric

2 buttons ⅝˝ to ¾˝ in diameter

Cutting

Patterns are on tissue paper pattern sheets.

Tana Lawn Print
    Cut 1 of pattern piece 12A for the lining.

Outer Fabric
    Cut 1 of pattern piece 12A for the case.

Heavyweight Interfacing
    Cut 1 rectangle 7½˝ × 10¼˝ for the flap.

    Cut 1 rectangle 9˝ × 10¼˝ for the body.

    Cut 1 rectangle 6˝ × 10¼˝ for the pocket.

Fusible Batting
    Cut 1 of pattern piece 12A for the case.

CONSTRUCTION

- *Fuse the polyester batting (12A) to the wrong side of the corresponding Tana Lawn fabric piece.*

- *Unless otherwise indicated, use a ½˝ seam allowance, sew all seams with the right sides of the fabric facing each other, and backstitch at the beginning and end of all seams.*

- *Top stitching, unless otherwise indicated, should be spaced ⅛˝ away from edges or seams.*

Sew

ASSEMBLE CASE

1. Mark pivot points on the wrong side of the lining fabric at each seamline corner ½˝ in from edges of corners.

2. Mark the top-stitching lines on the right side of the outer case fabric, across the shorter width of the case, as indicated on the pattern piece.

3. Sew the elastic loops to the outer canvas fabric, at the marks indicated on the pattern piece, leaving a ¾˝ to 1˝ loop section, depending on the button size, inside the seamline toward the center of the case.

> **TIP** *Knot one end of the hair elastic loop in an overhand knot, and place the knotted end on the seam allowance side of the stitching line. The knot will prevent the ends of the elastic from popping out of the seam should the elastic loop become separated.*

Sew hair elastics in place.

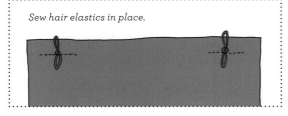

4. Pin the case lining on top of the outer case, right sides together, matching the shaped edges. Beginning at a large dot, start sewing in the seam allowance. Pivot when you arrive at the stitching line, and then continue sewing the seam. Pivot at each corner and stop sewing when you reach the other large dot. Pivot; sew out through the seam allowance and off the case layers. Repeat until you have sewn the entire perimeter of the case, leaving 3 separate openings in a long side.

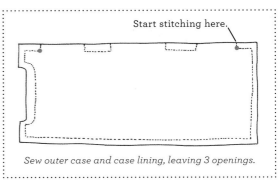

Start stitching here.

Sew outer case and case lining, leaving 3 openings.

5. Clip the excess seam allowance at each corner.

6. Turn the case right side out. Press.

7. Topstitch across the case on marked top-stitching lines 1 and 2, backstitching at the beginning and end of the stitching lines.

8. Insert each of the cut heavyweight interfacing sections into its corresponding case section through the opening in the seamline in each section. Bend the interfacing slightly to fit it through the smaller opening. Center the interfacing pieces in each section as best you can and fuse in place.

9. Topstitch line 3, through the flap end piece of heavyweight interfacing as well, to make the spine.

10. Topstitch the entire case edge, closing the open sections in the seam as you sew.

11. Sew the buttons onto the outside of the case at the marks indicated on the pattern piece.

12. Fold the shaped case edge up toward the main part of the case on the top-stitching line with the lining sides together. Topstitch along each short side to make the pocket. Backstitch at the beginning and end of the stitching line to reinforce the seam.

13. Give the case a final press, folding the flap down over the pocket.

Slide your device in the pocket, slide the loops onto the buttons, and enjoy the case!

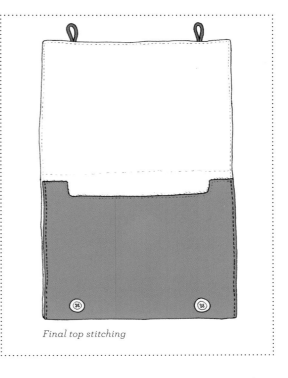

Final top stitching

AROUND TOWN
TOTE BAG

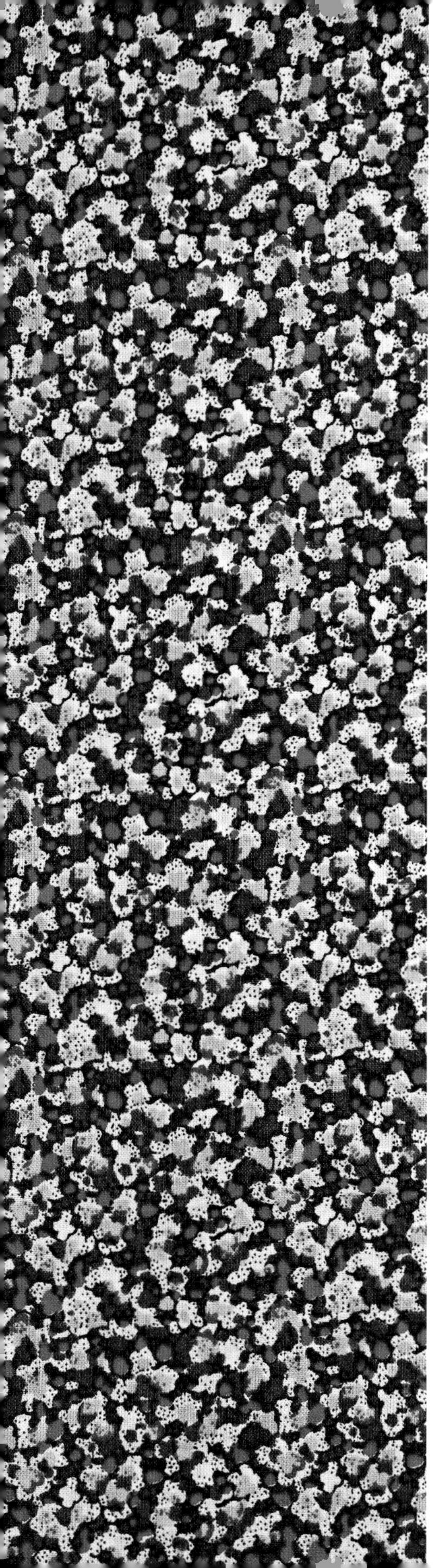

AROUND TOWN TOTE BAG

FINISHED SIZE: BAG 12″ WIDE × 15″ TALL, STRAPS 15″

With its classic lines and small size, this lightweight, casual bag can rest on your shoulder for a full day of errands. Each alternating stripe features the classic Liberty of London print Pepper and a gray-and-white microstripe. I repurposed a red patent leather belt for the straps, which are hand sewn onto the bag with heavy top-stitching thread.

This bag sews up quickly and requires only ¼ yard of the featured Liberty of London fabric. With some Liberty fat quarters or some fun fabrics from your stash, you could even make a scrappy version that uses a different print fabric for each stripe.

Supplies Needed

The fabrics shown here, paired with the Liberty Tana Lawn prints, are all woven, quilting weight, and 100% cotton.

- ¾ yard light gray fabric for outer bag and bag lining
- ¼ yard Liberty Tana Lawn for outer bag
- 1 yard lightweight fusible interfacing, 20″ wide (I use Shape-Flex.)
- ½ yard midweight fusible interfacing, 45″ wide (I use Pellon Décor Bond.)
- 1 magnetic snap
- 1 belt (measuring at least 40″ in the section without punched holes) for straps
- Heavy-duty top-stitching, upholstery, or button thread
- Metal awl with pointed tip
- Leather hand-sewing needle (also called a glover's needle)

Cutting

Tana Lawn Print

Cut 6 pieces 4″ × 14″ for outer bag stripes.

Outer and Lining Fabric

Cut 4 pieces 4″ × 14″ for outer bag stripes.

Cut 2 pieces 14″ × 18″ for lining.

Belt

Cut 2 sections, each 19″ long (free of any punched holes).

Lightweight Fusible Interfacing

Cut 10 pieces 4″ × 14″ for the outer bag stripes.

Midweight Fusible Interfacing

Cut 2 pieces 14″ × 18″.

CONSTRUCTION

- *Following the manufacturer's instructions, fuse lightweight interfacing to the wrong side of the corresponding Tana Lawn and cotton fabric pieces for outer bag stripes.*

- *Unless otherwise indicated, use a ½˝ seam allowance, sew all seams with the right sides of the fabric facing each other, and backstitch at the beginning and end of all seams.*

- *Top stitching, unless otherwise indicated, should be spaced ⅛˝ away from edges or seams.*

Sew

OUTER BAG

1. Using a ¼˝ seam allowance, sew fused outer bag strips together along the long edges, alternating fabrics. Begin and end with a Liberty print strip and continue until you have pieced 3 Liberty strips and 2 gray print strips. Press seam allowances open.

Sewn outer bag section

2. Topstitch to the left and right of each outer bag strip seam.

3. Following the manufacturer's instructions, fuse the midweight interfacing to the wrong side of the completed outer bag section.

4. Repeat Steps 1–3 with the remaining outer bag strips to make the other side.

Assemble Bag

1. Sew the 2 outer bag sections together at the sides and bottom, pivoting at the corners. Clip the excess seam allowances at each corner. Turn the bag right side out and press.

2. Following the manufacturer's instructions, install a side of the magnetic snap in each lining piece, centered from the sides and 2˝ down from the upper raw edge.

3. Sew the 2 lining pieces together at the sides and bottom, pivoting at the corners and leaving a 5˝ opening centered in the bottom seam.

4. Slip the outer bag into the bag lining, right sides together, aligning side seams and upper raw edges. Sew the upper edge seam of the bag in a continuous stitching line to create a finished edge. (Sew through only one outer bag layer and one lining layer at a time.) When you have sewn all the way around and you come back to the beginning of this seam, continue stitching about 1˝ or so to reinforce.

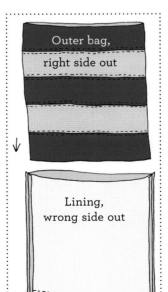

Outer bag, right side out

Lining, wrong side out

Wrong side of outer bag

Stitch.

Wrong side of lining

Sew upper bag seam.

Note: When sewing a seam around a tube shape (think of a pants leg, a shirt sleeve, or here, the upper seam of the bag), refer to your sewing machine manual to utilize the free-arm feature if it is offered. For most domestic machines, it is as easy as removing the accessory tray.

5. Turn the bag right side out through the opening in the lining. Leave the lining pulled up, away from the outer bag.

6. Topstitch the opening in the lower seam of the lining closed.

7. Push the lining down into the outer bag. Press.

8. Topstitch the upper seam edge of the bag.

Attach Handles

1. Use the pointed tip of the metal awl to pierce 2 sets of 4 holes at each end of the cut belt sections. Each set of 4 holes should form a ¼″ × ½″ rectangle, the holes being the corners of the rectangle.

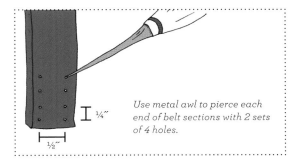

¼″

½″

Use metal awl to pierce each end of belt sections with 2 sets of 4 holes.

2. Mark the strap placement on the outer bag. Each mark should be 1⅝″ down from the top of the bag and 3″–4″ in from the side seam. This mark is the center of the pierced hole section of the strap.

3. Use a leather needle and a doubled strand of heavy-duty thread to sew the strap ends to the bag. Start on the inside of the bag and sew through both the lining and outer layers of the bag, making an X shape with the stitching in each of the boxes of holes prepunched with the awl. Note: Sew as if you are lacing tennis shoes to create the X-shaped stitches.

Give the tote bag a final press, avoiding the straps, and your bag is complete!

ALL ZIPPED
UP BAG

FINISHED SIZE: BAG 18˝ WIDE × 12˝ TALL × 5˝ DEEP, STRAP 28˝

This accommodating satchel features a long shoulder strap, a zippered main opening, and pieced side panels. For the alternating pieced panels I chose the classic Liberty of London print Edenham. The main bag exterior is metallic linen and the lining is a black and off-white dot print.

Supplies Needed

Paired with the Liberty Tana Lawn print, the outer fabric is midweight linen, the lining fabric is quilting-weight cotton, and all are woven.

1 yard metallic linen for outer bag

⅝ yard black print for bag lining

¼ yard Liberty Tana Lawn for outer bag piecing

3½ yards lightweight fusible interfacing (I use Shape-Flex.)

⅜ yard midweight double-sided fusible interfacing (I use fast2fuse.)

1 zipper, 17˝ long

2 swivel latch clips ¾˝

2 D-rings 1¼˝

Cutting

Template pattern is on tissue paper pattern sheets.

Tana Lawn Print

Fuse lightweight fusible interfacing to the back of the fabric before cutting.

Cut 34 of pattern piece MM triangle from *Marcelle Medallion Quilt*, Border 2.

Cut 2 pieces 1¼˝ × 4˝ for zipper tab ends.

Outer Fabric

Before cutting, fuse lightweight fusible interfacing to the back of enough fabric for the triangle pieces only.

Cut 34 of pattern piece MM triangle from *Marcelle Medallion Quilt*, Border 2.

Cut 2 pieces 11½˝ × 15½˝ for main bag.

Cut 4 pieces 3½˝ × 15½˝ for sides.

Cut 1 strip 3¾˝ × 32˝ for strap.

Cut 2 pieces 1¾˝ × 2˝ for D-ring tab.

Lining Fabric

Cut 2 pieces 20½˝ × 15½˝ for main bag lining.

Lightweight Fusible Interfacing

Cut 2 pieces 20½˝ × 15½˝ for main bag lining.

Cut 2 pieces 11½˝ × 15½˝ for main bag.

Cut 4 pieces 3½˝ × 15½˝ for sides.

Cut 1 strip 3¾˝ × 29˝ for strap.

Midweight Double-Sided Fusible Interfacing

Cut 2 pieces 15˝ × 4½˝ for bottom.

Cut 2 pieces 1˝ × 1¼˝ for D-ring tab.

CONSTRUCTION

- *Fuse lightweight interfacing to the wrong side of the corresponding outer bag and bag lining pieces. When fusing the long strap section, center the interfacing to allow for a 1½˝ section of fabric at each end without interfacing.*

- *Unless otherwise indicated, use a ½˝ seam allowance, sew all seams with the right sides of the fabric facing each other, and backstitch at the beginning and end of all seams.*

- *Top stitching, unless otherwise indicated, should be spaced ⅛˝ away from edges or seams.*

Sew

BAG BODY

1. Follow the *Marcelle Medallion Quilt*, Border 2 instructions (page 81) to piece the strips of MM triangles for the main bag panel. Piece all of the triangles into a single long strip. Cut the strip into 4 sections 15½˝ long.

2. Sew a pieced strip to each of the long edges of the main bag panel, matching outer bag fabrics and using a ¼˝ seam allowance. Press the seam allowances toward the main bag panel. Topstitch next to the seam, on the main bag panel.

3. Sew a 3½˝ × 15½˝ side piece to each long, pieced strip edge of the main bag panel. Press the seam allowances toward the side panel. Topstitch next to the seam, on the side panel.

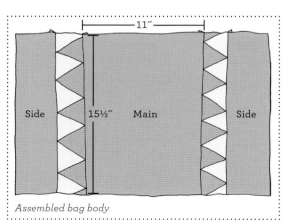

Assembled bag body

4. To place a dart on the upper edge of the main bag panel, mark a line on the wrong side from the center down 3˝. Mark ½˝ to either side along the upper edge. Connect these marks to the bottom of the 3˝ line.

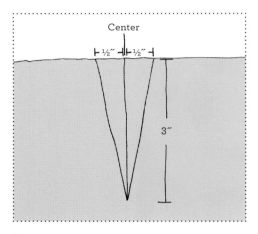

5. Fold fabric right sides together along the centerline. Pin and stitch along the outer line to mark the dart.

6. Repeat Steps 4 and 5 to mark and sew darts 2½˝ to either side of the center dart.

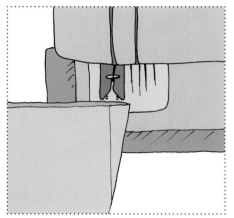

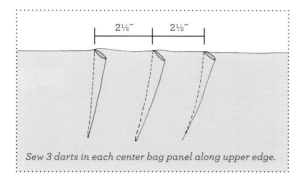

Sew 3 darts in each center bag panel along upper edge.

7. Repeat Steps 1–6 with the remaining pieced strips, main bag panel, and side panels.

ZIPPER

1. Sew the narrow side of a 1¼˝ × 4˝ zipper tab end to the right side of the zipper at each end of the zipper, through the zipper tape and tab fabric only. Press the tabs away from the zipper. Trim the zipper section to measure 20½˝ long.

2. Sandwich the zipper between the darted edge of an outer bag panel and a lining panel, with fabrics right sides together, and face (or right) side of zipper toward the right side of the outer fabric. Sew the length of the bag as shown, using a ¼˝ seam allowance.

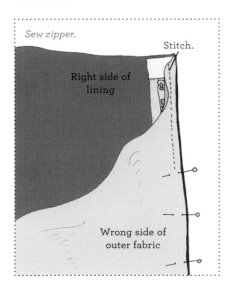

Sew zipper.

Stitch.

Right side of lining

Wrong side of outer fabric

3. Press the fabrics away from the zipper teeth and topstitch.

4. Repeat Steps 2 and 3 with the remaining outer bag panel and lining panel on the other side of the zipper tape.

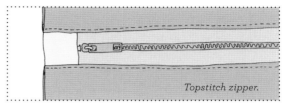

Topstitch zipper.

Assemble Bag

1. Open up the zipper, align the outer bag pieces, right sides together, and sew the side and lower edges. Start and stop stitching ½˝ below the zipper. Repeat with the lining pieces, this time starting at the bottom edge, leaving an 8˝ opening centered in the bottom of the lining.

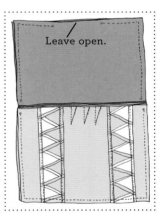

Leave open.

2. Cut 2½˝ × 2½˝ squares from the lower right and left corners of the outer bag and the lining.

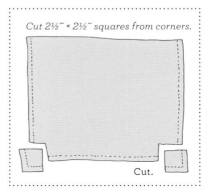

Cut 2½˝ × 2½˝ squares from corners.

Cut.

3. Open a cut corner. Press raw edges right sides together so that the side seam and lower bag seam are aligned. Sew across the aligned edges to create the flat bottom of the bag. Repeat with the remaining cut corners of lining and outer bag.

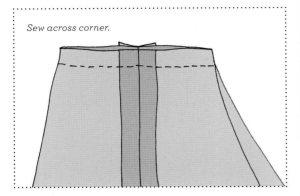

Sew across corner.

4. Turn the bag right side out through the opening in the lining. Push the outer bag inside the lining so that the lining is facing out. Push each of the upper corners of the bag to the inside, matching the center of the zipper to the side seam. Note: This is much like the way you just matched the lower corners to box them. Sew across the aligned edges with a ⅝˝ seam allowance. Trim the excess seam allowance down to ¼˝.

5. Slip the 2 layers of double-sided fusible interfacing into the bottom of the bag through the opening in the lining. Fuse them to the outer bag fabric only.

6. Topstitch the opening in the lower seam of the lining closed.

7. Turn the bag right side out. Fuse the interfacing in the bag bottom to the lining layer by placing the iron inside of the bag to fuse.

SEW D-RING TABS

1. Following the manufacturer's instructions to fuse the wrong side of the D-ring tab to the D-ring tab interfacing, wrap seam allowances around to the back of the interfacing and fuse in place. Topstitch the edges of the D-ring tab.

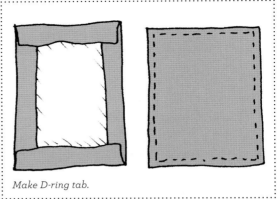

Make D-ring tab.

2. Centered on the side seam and 1½˝ below the finished upper edge, topstitch the lower edge of the D-ring tab to the side pieces, stitching a box ¾˝ wide × ⅜˝ tall in line with the lower (previously completed) top stitching.

3. Slide a D-ring onto the tab with the flat side between the tab and the bag side. Repeat the same type of top stitching as in Step 2 to sew the remaining free tab end to the bag.

4. Repeat Steps 1–3 with the remaining D-ring tab pieces and D-ring on the other side of the bag.

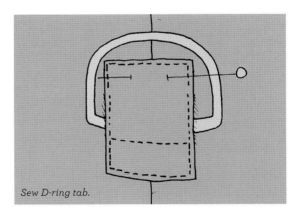

Sew D-ring tab.

Finish Bag

1. Fold the fused strap in half lengthwise, and press a crease. Fold the long cut edges in to the center crease. Press again.

2. Fold the strap in half lengthwise on the first pressed crease so that the raw edges are enclosed.

3. Topstitch the strap along the open, long side, a scant ⅛″ from the edge. Topstitch the remaining folded edge.

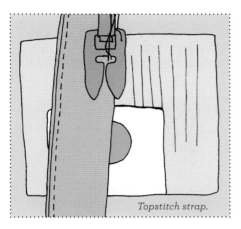

Topstitch strap.

4. Press the strap ends 1″ toward the wrong side. Turn under 1″ again.

5. Slip a swivel latch onto each of the strap ends. Topstitch the pressed edge of each strap end to the main strap section, trapping the hardware in the folded loop of the strap.

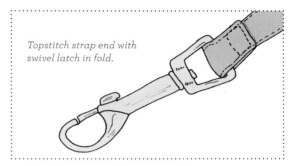

Topstitch strap end with swivel latch in fold.

6. Clip the strap latches to the D-rings at the bag sides.

Give the tote bag a final press, and your bag is complete!

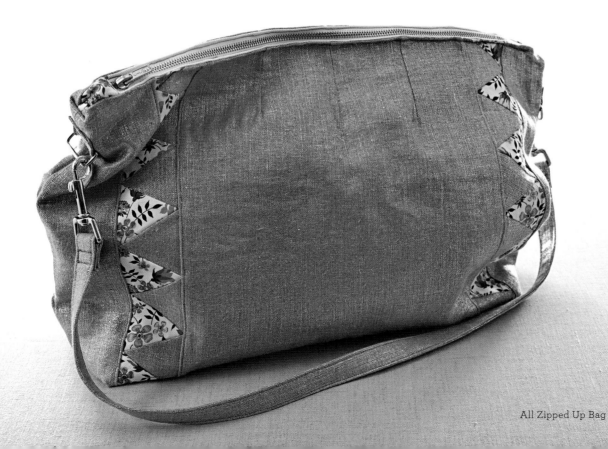

SEW AND GO ORGANIZER

This organizer has the perfect place for all of your sewing essentials. It has pockets for small notebooks or patterns, an embroidery scissor pocket, a chain to hold thread spools, and even some felt pages to hold hand-sewing needles. An airmail-style fabric envelope will secure the bits and pieces that can easily get away, and the stitched-in measuring tape will never get lost. The organizer even has its own tiny patchwork pincushion that snaps in and out.

FINISHED SIZE: WITH THE ORGANIZER OPEN 28˝ × 10½˝,
HANDLE LOOP 5˝

The main part of the organizer has durable heavyweight interfacing inside. The tie closure and wrap-around style keep everything contained.

Drawing from the French feel of the Liberty of London Phillipa print by Grayson Perry, I pulled a variety of red, white, gray, and blue prints for the organizer. I used a cream-and-blue cotton for the exterior, along with some red wool felt for the appliqué.

Supplies Needed

⅜ yard blue striped cotton fabric for organizer exterior

½ yard gray cotton print fabric for lining

1 fat quarter each of 2 quilting-weight cotton fabrics (a red and a blue) for interior pockets 1 and 2

1 fat quarter of Liberty Tana Lawn fabric for interior pocket 3

1 fat quarter red fabric for bias trim

¼ yard off-white fabric for envelope pocket 5

1 piece 3˝ × 6˝ of red wool felt cut into desired *sew* appliqué shape from template pattern

1 piece 2½˝ × 4˝ of off-white wool felt for needle book

⅛ yard fabric for scissor pocket 6 and handle loop

Small scraps for pincushion

½ yard heavyweight double-sided fusible interfacing (I use fast2fuse.)

⅜ yard midweight fusible interfacing (I use Pellon Décor Bond.)

1¾ yards of ¼˝-wide grosgrain ribbon cut into the following lengths: 9˝, 8˝, 8˝, 18˝, and 18˝

½ yard airmail envelope–style ¼˝-wide ribbon for pocket 5

10˝ white metal jewelry chain, ¼˝ wide

1 large metal snap

1 small metal snap

1 yellow vinyl or cloth measuring tape (Pry off the metal tab at the beginning of the tape and cut the tape on the 6˝ line.)

Polyester fiberfill

Optional: Use top-stitching thread and a suitable machine needle for all top-stitching steps.

Cutting

Patterns are on tissue paper pattern sheets.

Blue Striped Fabric

Cut 2 of pattern piece 8A for outer sides.

Cut 1 piece 8½˝ × 10½˝ for outer center panel.

Cut 2 pieces 2½˝ × 10½˝ for outer spine.

Gray Lining Fabric

Cut 2 of pattern piece 8A for inner sides.

Cut 1 piece 8½˝ × 10½˝ for inner center panel.

Cut 2 pieces 2½˝ × 10½˝ for inner spine.

Blue Pocket Fabric

Cut 2 pieces 8⅜˝ × 9½˝ for pocket 1 (inside left large pocket).

Red Pocket Fabric

Cut 2 pieces 7¾˝ × 8⅜˝ for pocket 2 (inside right medium pocket).

Liberty Print Pocket Fabric

Cut 1 and 1 reversed of pattern piece 9A for pocket 3 (inside lower left pocket).

Scissor Pocket and Handle Fabric

Cut 2 of pattern piece 10A for pocket 4 (inside left scissor pocket).

Cut 1 rectangle 3˝ × 13½˝ for handle loop.

Envelope Pocket Fabric

Cut 2 of pattern piece 11A for pocket 5 (center envelope pocket).

Fabric Scraps for Pincushion

Cut 7 squares 1¼˝ × 1¼˝ from dark print fabrics.

Cut 8 squares 1¼˝ × 1¼˝ from light print fabrics.

Cut 1 rectangle 2¾˝ × 4¼˝ for pincushion back.

Red Fabric

Cut into bias strips 2¼˝ wide. Piece shorter strips to make a continuous strip at least 76˝ long.

Midweight Fusible Interfacing

Cut 2 of pattern piece 8A for sides.

Cut 1 piece 8½˝ × 10½˝ for center panel.

Cut 2 pieces 2½˝ × 10½˝ for spine.

Cut 1 piece 8⅜˝ × 9½˝ for pocket 1.

Cut 1 piece 7¾˝ × 8⅜˝ for pocket 2.

Cut 1 of pattern piece 9A for pocket 3.

Cut 1 rectangle 3˝ × 13½˝ for handle loop.

Heavyweight Interfacing

Cut 2 of pattern piece 8A for side.

Cut 1 piece 8½˝ × 10½˝ for center panel.

Cut 2 pieces 2½˝ × 10½˝ for spine.

Cut 1 piece 2⅛˝ × 3½˝ for pincushion.

CONSTRUCTION

- *Unless otherwise indicated, use a ½˝ seam allowance, sew all seams with the right sides of the fabric facing each other, and backstitch at the beginning and end of all seams.*

- *Topstitching, unless otherwise indicated, should be spaced ⅛˝ away from edges or seams.*

Fuse Interfacing

Follow manufacturer's instructions to fuse all midweight interfacing pieces to the wrong side of their corresponding lining, strap, and pockets 1–3 fabric pieces.

Sew

CONSTRUCT PINCUSHION

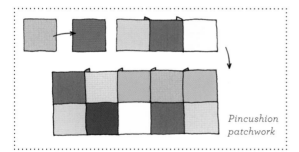

Pincushion patchwork

1. Using a ¼˝ seam allowance for all the pincushion seams, piece the patchwork for the pincushion top according to the diagram. Sew 3 rows of 5 squares, alternating light and dark fabrics. Press. Sew the 3 rows together. Press.

2. Sew the pincushion top and back right sides together. Leave a 2˝ opening in the seam, centered on a long side. Clip the excess seam allowances at each corner.

3. Turn the pincushion right side out. Insert the 2⅛˝ × 3½˝ piece of heavyweight interfacing into the opening, aligning it with the pincushion back.

4. Hand stitch the female side of the large snap through the pincushion back and interfacing.

5. Stuff the pincushion with fiberfill, placing the stuffing between the interfacing and the pincushion top. Do not overstuff.

6. Hand sew the pincushion opening closed, using a ladder stitch.

CONSTRUCT POCKETS

1. Sew 2 matching pocket 1 pieces together along the smaller side. Turn right side out and press. Topstitch along seam to finish the upper edge.

2. Repeat Step 1 to finish the upper edge of pockets 2 and 3.

3. Sew the pocket 4 pieces together as shown, and leave an opening as indicated on the pattern piece. Clip excess seam allowances at the corners. Turn right side out and press. Topstitch along the upper, finished seam edge.

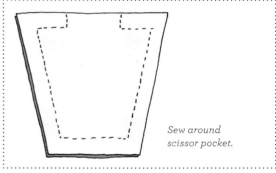

Sew around scissor pocket.

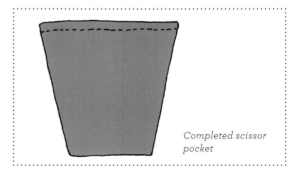

Completed scissor pocket

4. Topstitch pocket 4 along the lower 3 edges to pocket 3, using the placement line indicated on the pattern piece.

5. Sew the center of the 9˝ section of ribbon to the lower pocket, centered ¾˝ above the upper edge of the scissor pocket. Backstitch across the ¼˝ width of the ribbon a few times to secure.

6. Sew the 2 pocket 5 pieces together, leaving an opening as indicated on the pattern piece. Clip excess seam allowances at corners and turn right side out. Topstitch the triangular pointed end of the envelope seam and the opposite short end. Press the envelope on the fold lines indicated on the pattern piece, folding the short end up and the pointed edge down over it.

7. Hand sew the male side of the small snap to the inside envelope point, following the snap mark indicated on the pattern piece.

8. Hand sew the remaining side of the small snap to the outside fabric side at the other snap mark indicated on the pattern piece.

CONSTRUCT MAIN PANELS

1. Sew the outer panels in order, from left to right: side (8A) to spine, center panel to other side of spine, remaining spine to center panel, and then, with an end of an 18˝ ribbon section centered and trapped in the seam, the side to the other side of the spine. Press the seam allowances open. Set aside.

2. Baste pocket 3 on top of pocket 1 with the lower right edges aligned; then baste to the lining left side panel. Trim the lower left edge of the pockets in line with the curved edge of the side panel.

3. Baste pocket 2 to the lining right side panel with the lower left edges aligned. Trim the lower right edge of the pockets in line with the curved edge of the side panel.

4. Repeat Step 1 to construct the lining.

APPLIQUÉ

Place the felt appliqué *sew* on the right-hand side of the assembled outer main panel, parallel to the short side and spaced 1¼˝ in from all edges. Topstitch the appliqué in place through the center of each letter.

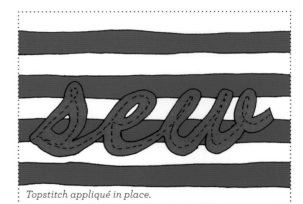

Topstitch appliqué in place.

SEW CENTER LINING PANEL ACCESSORIES

1. Place the 6″ section of measuring tape on the lining as marked on pattern piece 8A (align the top, bottom, and sides), and topstitch around the edges.

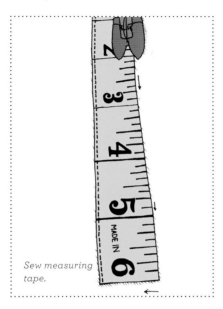

Sew measuring tape.

2. Leaving the triangular flap up out of the way, baste the folded lower edges of pocket 5 (envelope) to the lining as marked on pattern piece 8A.

3. Topstitch the airmail ribbon trim on top of the lower 3 (basted) edges of the envelope, folding the ends under and mitering the corners.

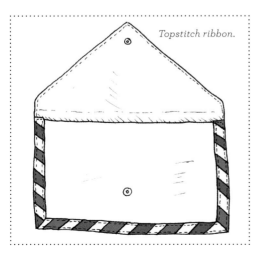

Topstitch ribbon.

4. Fold the wool felt in half widthwise. Place the folded edge on the lining along the placement line indicated on pattern piece 8A. Topstitch along the folded edge.

5. Sew the center of each 8″ section of ribbon to the lining on the right spine section, ¾″ from the upper and lower edges, backstitching across the ¼″ width of the ribbon a few times to secure.

6. Hand stitch the remaining side of the large snap to the lining as marked on the pattern piece.

Construct Organizer

1. Following the manufacturer's instructions, fuse the heavyweight double-sided fusible interfacing pieces to each of the corresponding outer and lining pieces by placing the interfacing between the fabrics with the wrong sides toward the interfacing. When fusing the interfacing to the inside panel, place a towel over the panel before ironing to protect the accessories.

2. Topstitch through all fused layers along the 2 spine seams.

3. Baste an end of an 18″ length of ribbon to the center of the left edge of the lining.

4. Fold the bias binding in half lengthwise. Press. Turn under ¾″ of a short end of the bias.

5. Sew the folded binding to the perimeter of the lining side of the organizer, raw edges aligned, with a ¼˝ seam allowance, beginning with the pressed end of the binding. When you get back to the beginning, overlap the end by 1˝, backstitch, and trim excess.

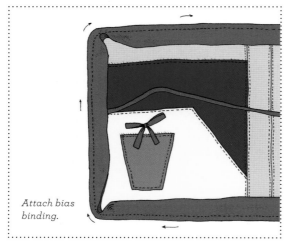

Attach bias binding.

6. Wrap the bias binding around the organizer edge, encasing the seam allowances. Topstitch (or stitch invisibly by hand) in place.

7. Slip the ends of the chain onto each of the stitched ribbons, and tie to secure.

SEW HANDLE LOOP

1. Press the 3˝ × 13½˝ handle loop rectangle in half lengthwise, wrong sides together, and make a crease. Fold the long edges in toward the center crease, spaced a scant ⅛˝ away from the crease, and press again.

2. Topstitch closed along the open, long side a scant ⅛˝ away from the edge. Topstitch the remaining (folded) edge.

3. Fold the raw ends of the topstiched strip under ½˝. Match the folded ends, and topstitch through all layers to the outer spine ⅜˝ and again ¾˝ from the upper edge to create the handle loop.

Now you can pack the organizer full of goodies!

QUEEN BEE
TOTE BAG

QUEEN BEE TOTE BAG

FINISHED SIZE: BAG 17½″ WIDE × 17″ TALL × 8″ DEEP, STRAPS 28″

This roomy tote can lug around your sewing machine, make a trip to the grocery store, or even house your handwork supplies at home. The scrappy hexagons are hand sewn using the English paper-piecing technique. The rugged construction of the main part of the bag, combined with the detail of the hexagon piecing, puts a modern spin on a traditional technique. If you love handwork, you will love making this sizable tote bag.

Because the patchwork uses small pieces of fabric, I delved into my vintage Liberty of London stash, cutting just a bit from a few special pieces. I mixed those with some new Liberty of London fabrics and new and vintage quilting fabrics, and combined them with a solid gray canvas. I hope this project inspires you to use some precious bits and pieces of fabrics you've been saving.

Supplies Needed

1¼ yards total various Liberty Tana Lawn and other cotton or cotton/linen print pieces for the hexagon patchwork (I used 24 different fabrics.)

1 yard gray cotton canvas for outer bag*

1½ yards quilting-weight cotton fabric for lining and bias

⅓ yard quilting-weight cotton fabric for interior pockets

1 magnetic snap

4 yards lightweight fusible interfacing, 20″ wide (I use Shape-Flex.)

2 yards midweight fusible interfacing, 45″ wide (I use Pellon Décor Bond.)

2 yards heavyweight double-sided fusible interfacing, 20″ wide (I use fast2fuse.)

138 lightweight card stock paper pieces cut from pattern piece 3A or 138 pieces 1½″ precut hexagon paper (#HEX150) from Paper Pieces (See Resources, page 159, for website.)

Optional: Use top-stitching thread and machine needle for all top-stitching steps.

* Requires 55″ usable width of fabric. If yours is narrower, you will need at least 1½ yards.

Cutting

Template is on tissue paper pattern sheets.

Prints for Hexagon Patchwork

Prepare the fabrics for cutting by fusing the light-weight fusible interfacing to the back of each fabric you will use for the hexagons.

Using a paper hexagon as a guide, cut 138 fused fabric pieces at least ¼˝ larger than the hexagon paper on all sides.

Cut hexagon pieces.

Gray Canvas

Cut 2 pieces 9˝ × 5½˝ for lower side panels.

Cut 2 pieces 18½ ˝ × 5½ ˝ for lower main panel.

Cut 1 piece 18½˝ × 9˝ for bottom.

Cut 2 pieces 3˝ × 10˝ for tab.

Cut 2 pieces 3½˝ × 54˝ for straps.

Optional: If you prefer shorter straps that you can carry with your hand, cut the straps and strap interfacing at 44˝ long.

Lining Fabric

Note: The lining pieces are cut 1˝ shorter than the outer bag panels to accommodate the bulk of the interfaced seams.

Cut 2 pieces 9˝ × 17˝ for side lining.

Cut 2 pieces 18½˝ × 17˝ for main lining.

Cut 1 piece 18½˝ × 9˝ for lining bottom.

Cut and piece together bias strips to make a length of binding 2¼˝ × 55˝.

Pocket Fabric

Cut 4 pieces 9˝ × 11˝ for interior side pockets.

Midweight Fusible Interfacing

Cut 2 pieces 3½˝ × 54˝ for strap.

Cut 2 pieces 3˝ × 10˝ for tab.

Cut 2 pieces 18½ ˝ × 9˝ for bottom.

Cut 2 pieces 9˝ × 5½˝ for lower side panels.

Cut 2 pieces 18½˝ × 5½˝ for lower main panels.

Cut 2 pieces 9˝ × 17˝ for side lining.

Cut 2 pieces 18½˝ × 17˝ for main lining.

Cut 2 pieces 18½˝ × 13½˝ for main hexagon panel.

Cut 2 pieces 9˝ × 13½˝ for side hexagon panel.

Heavyweight Interfacing

Cut 2 pieces 9˝ × 18˝ for sides.

Cut 2 pieces 18½˝ × 18˝ for main panel.

Cut 1 piece 18½˝ × 9˝ for bottom.

CONSTRUCTION

- *Unless otherwise indicated, use a ½˝ seam allowance, sew all seams with the right sides of the fabric facing each other, and backstitch at the beginning and end of all seams.*

- *Topstitching, unless otherwise indicated, should be spaced ⅛˝ away from edges or seams.*

Fuse Interfacing

Fuse all midweight interfacing pieces to the wrong side of their corresponding lining fabric and outer canvas fabric pieces.

HEXAGON PATCHWORK

1. Center a paper hexagon on the wrong side of a cut hexagon fabric piece and pin them together. Fold the seam allowance down over the paper piece and baste in place around the hexagon shape using long hand stitches. Leave 1˝ thread tails at the beginning and end of basting.

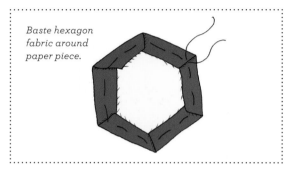

Baste hexagon fabric around paper piece.

2. Repeat Step 1 with all of the hexagon fabrics and paper pieces.

3. On a design wall or flat surface, arrange the hexagons for the main bag panels and the side bag panels:

Make 2 side panels with 6 rows of 4 hexagons each, using 24 hexagons in each.

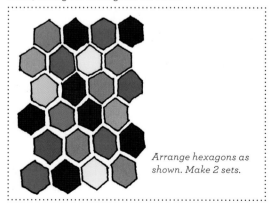

Arrange hexagons as shown. Make 2 sets.

Make 2 main panels with 6 rows of 8 and 7 hexagons alternately, using 45 hexagons in each.

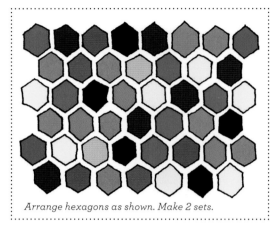

Arrange hexagons as shown. Make 2 sets.

4. Sew the hexagons together row by row. Whipstitch the pieces together at their side edges across the row.

5. Sew the rows of hexagons together. Complete all hexagon patchwork panels.

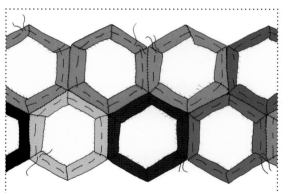

Whipstitch 2 rows together. Continue adding rows until all rows in panel are sewn.

6. Press the panels and remove all basting and paper pieces.

7. Cut the side panels down to 9˝ × 13½˝.

8. Cut the main panels down to 18½˝ × 13½˝.

9. Following the manufacturer's instructions, fuse the corresponding pieces of midweight fusible interfacing to all 4 hexagon panels.

CONSTRUCT STRAPS

1. Press a strap in half lengthwise and make a crease. Fold the long, cut edges in to the center crease. Press.

2. Topstitch the strap along the open, long side. Topstitch the remaining long side of the strap.

3. Repeat Steps 1 and 2 with the remaining strap.

CONSTRUCT OUTER BAG

1. Baste the strap ends in place 4½˝ from the side edge onto a long side of the lower main canvas panel. Repeat with the remaining strap and lower main canvas panel. The edge you baste the straps to will become the upper edge of the panel.

2. Sew the upper edge of a lower main canvas panel to the lower edge of a large hexagon panel. Press the seam down toward the canvas section and the straps up toward the hexagon panel. Topstitch the seam on the canvas side, stitching through the pressed seam allowances. Repeat with the remaining lower main canvas panel and large hexagon panel.

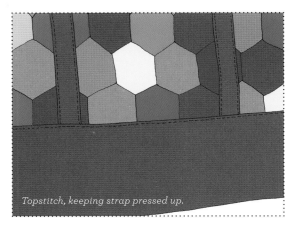

Topstitch, keeping strap pressed up.

3. Sew the upper edge of a lower side canvas panel to the lower edge of a small hexagon panel.

Press the seam down toward the canvas section. Topstitch the seam on the canvas side, stitching through the pressed seam allowances. Repeat with the remaining lower side canvas panel and the smaller hexagon panel.

4. Fuse each heavyweight fusible interfacing piece to its corresponding outer bag section.

5. Topstitch the strap to the main bag panel. Begin at the canvas seam and sew up toward the top of the bag, stopping 10˝ away. Turn and stitch across the strap, backstitching to reinforce. Turn and continue stitching back toward the canvas seam, ending the top stitching at the seamline.

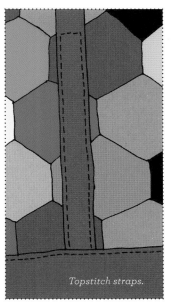

Topstitch straps.

6. On the wrong side, mark a dot at each lower corner seamline of the outer bag pieces and bag lining pieces. Each dot should be ½˝ from the corner of each piece.

7. Sew the lower edge of the outer side panel to a short side of the outer bag bottom from dot to dot. Repeat with the remaining outer side panel. Note: Be sure to backstitch at the beginning and end of each of the seams that construct this bag.

8. Sew the side edge of the outer main panel to the side edge of the bag side panel from upper edge to dot. Sew the remaining side edge of the outer main panel to the opposite bag side panel from upper edge to dot. Repeat with the remaining main bag panel and unsewn bag side edges.

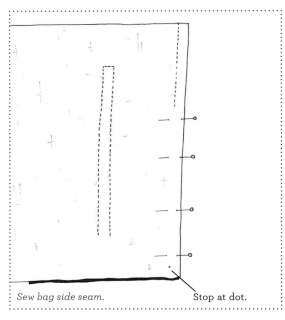

Sew bag side seam.   Stop at dot.

9. Sew the lower edge of the main bag panel to the long side of the bag bottom from dot to dot. Repeat with the remaining main bag panel lower edge and the bag bottom.

CONSTRUCT LINING

1. Sew 2 pocket pieces together along the 9˝ side. Turn right side out. Press. Topstitch the seam. Repeat with the 2 remaining pocket pieces.

2. Baste the pocket to the lining side panel, aligning the side and lower raw edges. Repeat with the remaining pocket and lining side panel.

3. Sew the lower edge of the lining side panel to a short side of the lining bottom from dot to dot. Repeat with the remaining lining side panel.

4. Sew the side edge of the lining main panel to the side edge of the lining side panel from dot to dot. Sew the remaining short side to the opposite lining side panel from dot to dot. Repeat with the remaining lining main panel and unsewn lining side edges.

5. Sew the lower edge of the lining main panel to the long side of the lining bottom from dot to dot. Repeat with the remaining lining main panel lower edge and the lining bottom.

INSTALL SNAP AND SEW TAB

1. Mark the magnetic snap placement on the right side of the tab piece and the outer bag piece. The snap mark on the outer bag should be centered between the straps 2½˝ down from the upper edge. The snap mark on the tab should be centered and 1½˝ from a short side, which will now be the lower edge of the tab. Take a moment to decide which side will be the front of the outer bag, where the tab will snap.

2. Install the magnetic snap onto the tab piece and the outer bag piece where marked.

3. Sew the sides and lower seam of the tab pieces. Clip the excess seam allowance at the lower corners and turn right side out. Press. Topstitch finished tab edges.

4. Baste the raw tab edges to the main outer bag on the opposite side of the magnetic snap, with the plain side of the tab facing the right side of the main outer bag.

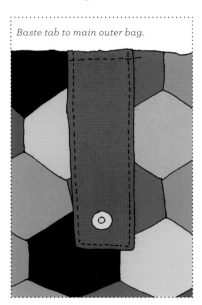

Baste tab to main outer bag.

Finish

1. Place the bag lining inside the outer bag, matching seams, and baste the upper raw edges of the outer bag and bag lining together. Keep the straps free of this stitching.

2. Press the binding in half lengthwise to make a crease. Open, then fold a long edge toward the center, about ⅛˝ from the crease. Press. Fold the other long edge toward the center, about ¼˝ away from the crease. Press.

3. Beginning along the center of the back side of the bag, sew the binding to the upper edge of the bag, following the crease line as the stitching line, with the deeper folded edge right sides together with the outside of the bag. Fold the binding, wrapping up and over the raw edges of the bag, to the inside of the bag and hand sew the folded edge of the binding to the lining.

4. Fold under the short end of the binding where it overlaps the beginning of the binding and stitch closed invisibly.

5. Give your bag a final press to fuse the wrong side of the lining to the double-sided fusible interfacing.

CLASSIC QUILTED HANDBAG

CLASSIC QUILTED HANDBAG

FINISHED SIZE: BAG 9″ WIDE × 6″ TALL × 2″ DEEP, STRAP 40″

Inspired by classic diminutive handbags, this quilted, cross-body bag has a chain strap and a zippered closure. In keeping with the timeless look, I chose classic Liberty of London prints for the outside of each bag. For the darker bag I used the classic Edenham print in deep navy with pops of red, green, pink, and blue paired with an Anna Maria Horner red floral print lining. For the light bag I used the classic Felicite print in soft pinks and lavender paired with a black-and-white polka dot lining.

Supplies Needed

⅓ yard Liberty Tana Lawn for outer bag

¼ yard quilting-weight cotton fabric for lining

1 package (3 yards) double-fold binding to match lining fabric

40″ length of purse chain

1 tassel with loop

1 zipper 9″ long

Hera marker

¼ yard lightweight fusible polyester batting (I use Pellon Fusible Fleece.)

½ yard heavyweight double-sided fusible interfacing (I use fast2fuse.)

24″-long quilting ruler with 45° markings

Cutting

Patterns are on tissue paper pattern sheets.

Tana Lawn Print

Cut 1 piece 1⅛″ × width of fabric for strap.

Cut 1 piece 9″ × 40″ to be quilted.

Lining Fabric

Cut 2 of pattern piece 1A for main lining.

Cut 1 piece 3″ × 7″ for bottom.

Cut 2 pieces 1⅝″ × 10″ for zipper panels.

Cut 2 pieces 3″ × 7½″ for sides.

Heavyweight Double-Sided Fusible Interfacing

Cut 2 of pattern piece 1A Bag Body.

Cut 1 piece 3″ × 7″ for bottom.

Cut 2 pieces 1⅝″ × 10″ for zipper panels.

Cut 2 pieces 3″ × 7½″ for sides.

Lightweight Fusible Polyester Batting

Cut 1 piece 9″ × 40″.

QUILTING OUTER BAG FABRIC

Fuse polyester batting to the wrong side of the corresponding Tana Lawn fabric piece.

Mark for Quilting

1. Referring to Diamond Grid Instructions (page 41), align the 45° line on the ruler with the long cut edge of the fabric, and mark the fabric with the Hera marker.

2. Continue, marking each row 1″ from the previous row until you have covered the entire width of the fabric with lines 1″ apart in both directions to create a diamond pattern.

Quilt

Machine quilt using straight-line quilting and following the marked lines.

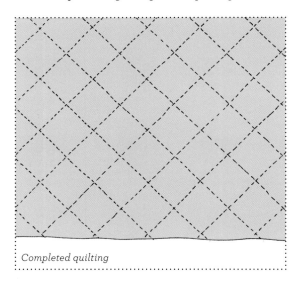

Completed quilting

Cut

Quilted Tana Lawn Print

Cut 2 of pattern piece 1A Bag Body.

Cut 1 rectangle 3″ × 7″ for the bottom.

Cut 2 rectangles 1⅝″ × 10″ for zipper panels.

Cut 2 rectangles 3″ × 7½″ for side pieces.

CONSTRUCTION

- *Unless otherwise indicated, use a ½˝ seam allowance, sew all seams with the right sides of the fabric facing each other, and backstitch at the beginning and end of all seams.*

- *Topstitching, unless otherwise indicated, should be spaced ⅛˝ away from edges or seams.*

Sew

CONSTRUCT STRAP

1. Press the strap in half lengthwise to make a crease. Fold the long cut edges toward the center crease, keeping the strap folded on the original pressed crease so that the raw edges are encased. Press again.

2. Topstitch strap along the open, long side a scant ⅛˝ from the edge.

3. Cut 2 sections 1½˝ long from the strap and set aside to create the strap loops.

4. Thread the strap through the purse chain, weaving in and out every other link. Make sure the chain is fully extended and is not gathering onto the strap as you thread it through.

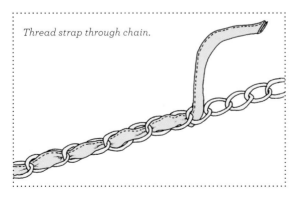

Thread strap through chain.

T I P *After you have the strap woven through the chain, it is a good time to test the length and trim away any excess chain or strap as needed.*

5. Thread each of the 1½˝ strap loop sections through the last links of the chain and fold them together, aligning the cut ends. Baste the strap ends and the cut ends of the strap loop sections together.

INSERT ZIPPER

1. With the zipper closed, sandwich a long edge of the zipper tape between the outer bag zipper panel and the lining zipper panel, right sides together. Sew, using a ⅜˝ seam allowance. Press the fabrics away from the zipper teeth.

2. Open up the outer and lining sections and slide the zipper panel heavyweight interfacing pieces between them. Fuse in place following the manufacturer's instructions. Trim away any excess interfacing that extends beyond the fabric edges.

3. Topstitch next to the zipper through the outer fabric, interfacing, and lining layers. Repeat with the remaining zipper panels.

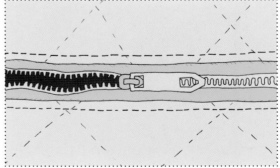

Sew zipper to zipper panels.

Construct Outer Bag

1. Sandwich each of the heavyweight fusible interfacing pieces between its corresponding outer bag section and lining section.

Optional: You can trim away the seam allowances of the interfacing pieces so that as you sew you will be sewing through only the outer quilted fabric and the lining fabric pieces. Fuse to the wrong sides of both fabrics according to the manufacturer's instructions.

2. Sew the short edge of a 3˝ × 7½˝ side bag section to the bag bottom. Press the seam allowance open.

3. Topstitch to the left and right of the seam, stitching through the seam allowances.

4. Repeat Steps 2 and 3 with the remaining side bag section.

5. Baste an end of the bag strap and strap loops to the upper edge of the bag side at the center.

6. Sew the short end of the completed zipper section to the upper edge of the bag side. Press the seam allowance open.

7. Topstitch the seam on the bag side section as you did in Step 3.

8. Repeat Steps 5–7 with the remaining short end of the zipper section and the opposite bag side section.

9. Unzip the zipper and turn the completed bag side/bottom/zipper section wrong side out.

10. Sew the bag side/bottom/zipper section to the main bag panels, matching notches to corresponding seamlines. Note: To make the straight edges of the bag side/bottom/zipper section curve around the main bag panels, you may want to clip just into the seam allowances of the side/bottom/zipper panels so that they will spread apart and conform to the curves.

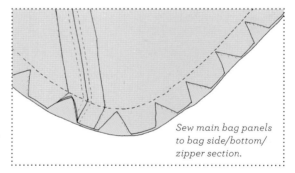

Sew main bag panels to bag side/bottom/zipper section.

Finish

1. Notch the seam allowance around the curved sections of the seams.

2. Sew the double-fold binding to the seam allowances around the bag body using a zigzag stitch and encasing the raw edges of the bag. Overlap binding at the ends.

3. Turn the bag right side out, through the zipper opening.

4. Attach the tassel to the zipper pull. Give the bag a final press, and it's finished!

A CLOSET FULL OF LIBERTY

FINISHED SIZE: 55″ LONG × 1⅞″ AT THE WIDEST POINT

Inspired by my grandfather Walter's ties, this skinny tie would make a wonderful gift. It is quite simple to sew. I used the classic Liberty of London print Edenham and lined the ends of the tie with a cotton voile floral print.

Supplies Needed

⅞ yard Liberty Tana Lawn

1⅛ yards 20″-wide lightweight fusible interfacing (I use Bi-Stretch Lite by Pellon.)

¾ yard tie interfacing

Note: Tie interfacing comes in many widths. At a minimum you need 40″ wide; if wider, you still need ¾ yard, but you will probably be able to cut more than one tie from the yardage.

Cutting

Patterns are on tissue paper pattern sheets.

Tana Lawn Print

   Cut 1 of pattern piece W35 Front.

   Cut 1 of pattern piece W36 Back.

   Cut 1 of pattern piece W37 Front Tipping.

   Cut 1 of pattern piece W38 Back Tipping.

Lightweight Fusible Interfacing

Note: Disregard grainline markings on pattern piece when cutting interfacing. Cut the pieces however they will fit on the yardage.

   Cut 1 of pattern piece
   W35 Front.

   Cut 1 of pattern piece
   W36 Back.

Tie Interfacing

   Cut 1 of pattern piece W39 Front Tie Interfacing.

   Cut 1 of pattern piece W40 Back Tie Interfacing.

CONSTRUCTION

Unless otherwise indicated, use a ½˝ seam allowance, sew all seams with the right sides of the fabric facing each other, and backstitch at the beginning and end of all seams.

Sew

1. Following the manufacturer's instructions, fuse the lightweight fusible interfacing pieces to the wrong side of the corresponding tie fabric pieces.

2. Sew the Front Tipping (W37) to the pointed end of the Front (W35), right sides together, on the stitching line indicated on W37. Clip seam allowances and turn right side out.

3. Repeat Step 2 with the Back (W36) and Back Tipping (W38).

4. Sew the Front (W35) to the Back (W36) along the narrow angled ends, offsetting ends by the width of the seam allowance to align pieces properly. Set aside.

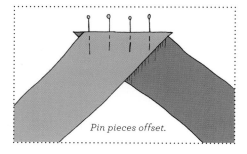

Pin pieces offset.

5. Sew the Front and Back Tie Interfacing pieces (W39 and W40) together with a zigzag stitch using an abutted (not overlapped) seam.

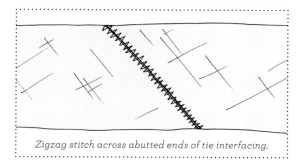

Zigzag stitch across abutted ends of tie interfacing.

6. With the wrong side of the tie facing up, fold a long edge of the tie ½˝ to the wrong side. Press.

7. Nest the points of the joined tie interfacing piece into the stitched tips on the body of the tie, centering the tie interfacing on top of the wrong side of the body of the tie. Baste or pin the tie interfacing to the center of the tie.

8. Fold the side of the tie without the ½˝ fold over the edge of the tie interfacing toward the center. Press.

9. Fold the ½˝ pressed edge of the tie over the raw edge of the tie fabric (the finished tie should be just a scant bit wider than the tie interfacing). Hand sew the center back seam using a slip stitch to create a lapped seam.

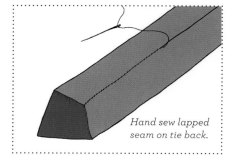

Hand sew lapped seam on tie back.

Give the tie a press and it is ready for wearing or giving!

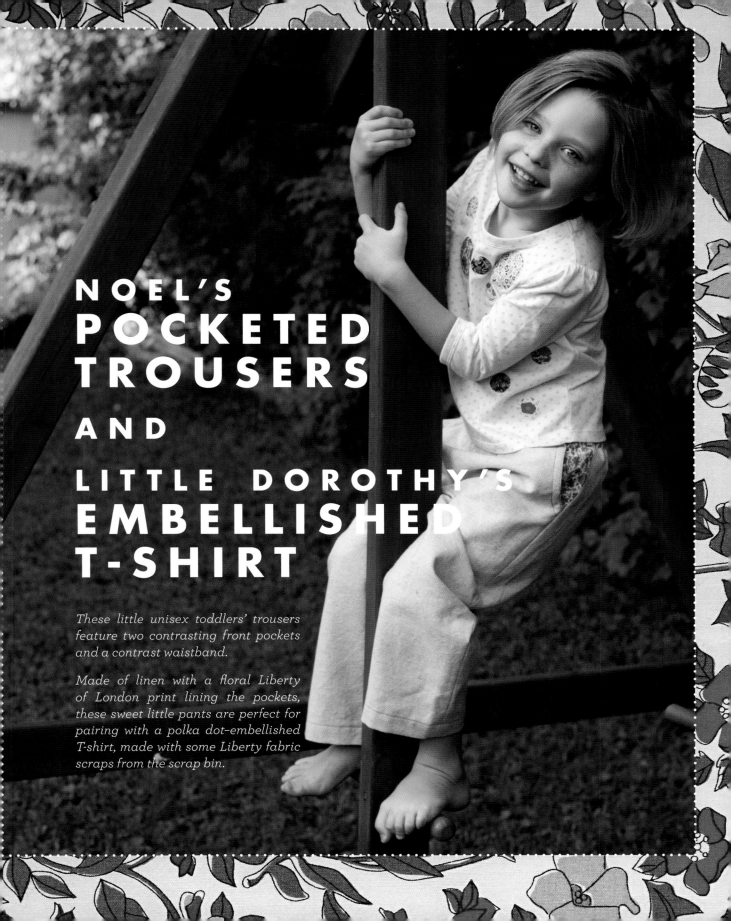

NOEL'S POCKETED TROUSERS

AND

LITTLE DOROTHY'S EMBELLISHED T-SHIRT

These little unisex toddlers' trousers feature two contrasting front pockets and a contrast waistband.

Made of linen with a floral Liberty of London print lining the pockets, these sweet little pants are perfect for pairing with a polka dot–embellished T-shirt, made with some Liberty fabric scraps from the scrap bin.

Supplies Needed

PANTS

Refer to the infants/toddlers size chart (page 158).

For all sizes

¼ yard Liberty Tana Lawn

1 yard ¾˝-wide nonroll or waistband elastic

⅛ yard of lightweight fusible interfacing (I use Pellon Bi-Stretch Lite.)

X-small (12–18 months)

¾ yard linen or other bottom-weight fabric

Small (18–24 months)

¾ yard linen or other bottom-weight fabric

Medium (3)

⅞ yard linen or other bottom-weight fabric

Large (4)

1 yard linen or other bottom-weight fabric

EMBELLISHED T-SHIRT

Variety of 4˝ × 4˝ scraps of Liberty Tana Lawn or other cotton fabric

⅓ yard double-sided fusible web for appliqué (I prefer Steam-A-Seam 2.)

T-shirt in the desired size

6-strand embroidery floss for stitching appliqués

Hand-sewing needle for stitching appliqués (I prefer a milliner's needle in size 5.)

Cutting

- *Patterns are on tissue paper pattern sheets.*

- *Refer to cutting layout at right and cut on folded fabric to cut 1 and 1 reversed of each piece that requires two pieces.*

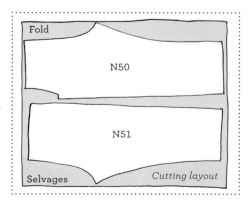

Cutting layout

CONSTRUCTION

Cutting, continued

Linen or Bottom-Weight Fabric

Cut 2 of pattern piece N50 Pants Front.

Cut 2 of pattern piece N51 Pants Back.

Tana Lawn Print

Cut 2 of pattern piece N52 Pocket Facing.

Cut 2 of pattern piece N53 Pocket Back.

Cut 1 of pattern piece N54 Waistband on fold.

Lightweight Fusible Interfacing

Cut 4 of pattern piece N55 Pocket Interfacing.

Elastic

Cut 1 length of elastic to the length listed according to size and your preferred fit.

Note: If you are making the trousers for a child you can measure, cut the elastic 1˝ smaller than the child's waist measurement to allow for a soft, snug fit of the elastic. If you want the elastic to barely hug the child's tummy, cut the elastic ½˝ larger than the waist measurement.

XS: 19½˝ **S:** 20˝ **M:** 20½˝ **L:** 21˝

- Unless otherwise indicated, use a ½˝ seam allowance, sew all seams with the right sides of the fabric facing each other, and backstitch at the beginning and end of all seams.

- Topstitching, unless otherwise indicated, should be spaced ⅛˝ away from edges or seams.

Sew

SEW POCKETS

1. Following the manufacturer's instructions, fuse the Pocket Interfacing (N55) to the wrong side of each Pants Front (N50) piece and each Pocket Facing (N52) piece along the curved pocket seam edge.

2. Sew the fused Pocket Facings and Pants Front pieces together along the curved pocket seam edges. Clip and notch the curved seam allowances. Turn the Pocket Facings to the inside of the Pants Fronts. Press.

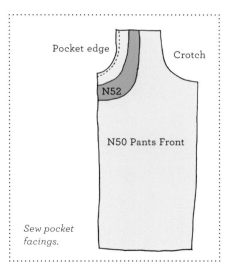

Pocket edge

Crotch

N52

N50 Pants Front

Sew pocket facings.

3. Topstitch the finished edges of the pocket seams, making sure to sew through both layers of the Pocket Facings.

Note: I think it looks nice to sew two rows of top stitching here, one just inside the edge and another about ⅜˝ down from the edge.

4. Pin the Pocket Backs (N53) to the Pocket Facings (N52) on the Pants Fronts (N50), right sides together, aligning top and side edges. Sew together along the outer curved edges to close the pocket.

ASSEMBLE PANTS

1. Sew the right Pants Front (N50) to the right Pants Back (N51) at the side seam and inseam. Repeat with the left pant leg pieces. Press. Be sure to catch the pocket side seam in the trouser side seam!

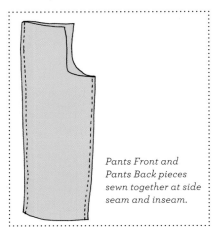

Pants Front and Pants Back pieces sewn together at side seam and inseam.

2. Turn a pant leg right side out and place it inside the other pant leg, which is still wrong side out. Sew the center pant seam from front to back, matching the inseams and notches. Press. It's a good idea to reinforce this seam by stitching again a scant ¼″ into the seam allowance.

3. Pin the short ends of the waistband right sides together. Sew ½″, leave a ⅝″ opening to insert the elastic later, and then sew the remainder of the seam. Press the seam allowances open.

4. Fold the waistband in half lengthwise, wrong sides together, on the fold line indicated on the pattern piece. Press. The side with the opening for the elastic will be the inside, or wrong side, of the waistband.

5. Pin the folded waistband around the top of the pants, right sides together and raw edges aligned, with the elastic opening facing out at the center

back. Sew the upper seam all the way around the pants. Pull the waistband up and press the seam allowance down toward the pant legs.

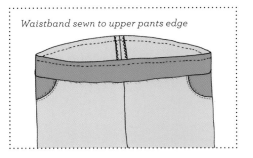

Waistband sewn to upper pants edge

T I P *When threading elastic through a casing, it is easy to accidentally pull the remaining free end of the elastic into the casing when you are close to the end. You then have to start over and rethread! To prevent this from happening, safety pin the remaining hanging end of the elastic to the pants next to the casing opening. You'll never have to rethread because the end of the elastic slipped into the casing!*

6. Using a bodkin or safety pin, thread the elastic through the casing. Take care not to twist the elastic inside the casing. When you come to the end, pull the ends of the elastic out of the opening and overlap them by 1″. Sew the ends together with a lapped seam, stitching back and forth across the elastic a few times to secure.

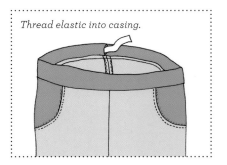

Thread elastic into casing.

7. Stretch the waistband to slide the remaining elastic back into the casing. I like to leave that small opening so the elastic can easily be adjusted.

8. Hem the trousers 1½˝.

ASSEMBLE T-SHIRT

1. Follow the manufacturer's instructions to apply the double-sided fusible web to the wrong side of the fabric scraps. (With Steam-A-Seam 2, you just need to press the web in place.)

2. Trace and cut as many appliqué pieces as you would like from the circle patterns on the tissue paper pattern sheets.

3. Fuse the fusible webbing side of each cut appliqué to the right side of the T-shirt.

4. Sew around the edge of each appliqué with a running stitch using 2 strands of embroidery thread.

Press this little ensemble, and it is ready to wear!

LITTLE PEARL DRESS

Inspired by classic children's dresses from the 1960s, this simple A-line dress has the same ruffled embellishment as the Michelle My Belle dress (page 143). And what little girl doesn't want to dress up just like Mommy? Sewn up in the classic Liberty of London print Mirabelle, this dress is as sweet as a little pink meringue.

This dress is quite simple to sew. With buttons down the back and a soft lining, this dress could become a staple to outfit your little one.

Supplies Needed

Refer to the infants/toddlers' size chart (page 158).

FABRIC

X-small (12–18 months)

⅝ yard Liberty Tana Lawn

⅝ yard lining fabric (I prefer cotton lawn or batiste.)

1 strip 2¼˝ × 12˝ of fabric for contrasting ruffle

Small (18–24 months) or Medium (3)

¾ yard Liberty Tana Lawn

¾ yard lining fabric (I prefer cotton lawn or batiste.)

1 strip 2¼˝ × 12˝ of fabric for contrasting ruffle

Large (4)

1 yard Liberty Tana Lawn

¾ yard lining fabric (I prefer cotton lawn or batiste.)

1 strip 2¼˝ × 12˝ of fabric for contrasting ruffle

OTHER SUPPLIES

3 pearl buttons with a shank ¼˝ wide

7 flat buttons ⅜˝ or ½˝ wide

6˝ pieces ⅝˝-wide ribbon (I prefer cotton or silk satin, rayon seam binding, or rayon grosgrain.)

Cutting

Patterns are on tissue paper pattern sheets. Refer to the cutting layout below to place the pattern pieces.

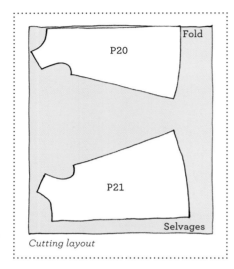

Cutting layout

Tana Lawn Print

Cut 1 of pattern piece P20 Dress Front on fold.

Cut 2 of pattern piece P21 Dress Back.

Lining Fabric

Cut 1 of pattern piece P20 Dress Front on fold.

Cut 2 of pattern piece P21 Dress Back.

CONSTRUCTION

- *Unless otherwise indicated, use a ½˝ seam allowance, sew all seams with the right sides of the fabric facing each other, and backstitch at the beginning and end of all seams.*

- *Topstitching, unless otherwise indicated, should be spaced ⅛˝ away from edges or seams.*

Sew

1. Using the print fabric, sew the Dress Front (P20) to the Dress Back (P21) at the shoulder seams. Repeat with the lining fabric pieces.

2. Sew the outer dress to the dress lining at the neck and armhole seams.

Wrong side of lining

Dress sewn to lining at neck and armhole seams

3. Clip and notch curved seam allowances and turn right side out by pulling the back pieces through the shoulder seams. Press.

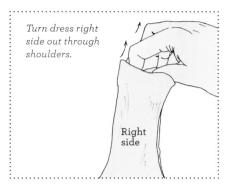

Turn dress right side out through shoulders.

Right side

4. Align the side seam at the underarm hole seam, and pull the lining away from the outer dress. Match the lining to the lining and the outer fabric to the outer fabric, and sew each side seam in a single continuous seam. Press.

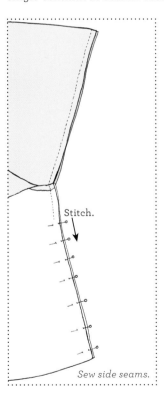

Stitch.

Sew side seams.

5. Hem dress ⅝˝ and hem lining ¾˝.

6. To finish the back edges of the dress, match the raw edges of the left side of the dress back and lining back, right sides together. Pin and stitch from the neck edge down to the hem. Turn right side out and press. Repeat with the remaining raw edges on the right-hand side of the dress.

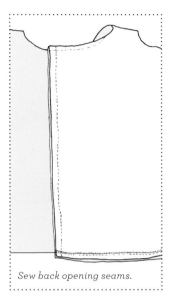

Sew back opening seams.

Finish

1. Sew 7 horizontal buttonholes, corresponding to the button size you chose, in the back right section of the dress through both layers of fabric. Place button holes ⅜˝ in from the finished back opening. Place the first buttonhole ½˝ down from the finished neck edge and last buttonhole 3˝ up from the finished hem edge. Space the remaining 5 buttonholes evenly between the top and bottom buttonhole. For size XS buttonholes are marked on the pattern piece.

2. Sew the 7 buttons onto the left back opening of the dress ¾˝ from the finished edge and use the buttonhole placement as a guide to space the buttons.

3. Finish all the raw edges of the 2¼˝ × 12˝ piece of fabric for the ruffle with a narrow zigzag stitch. Turn under ½˝ at the upper edge of the ruffle and press. Sew 2 rows of long basting stitches down the center of the ruffle, leaving long thread tails at each end. Fold and press the other end under ½˝.

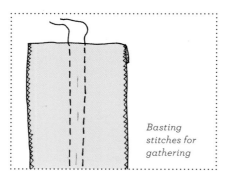

Basting stitches for gathering

4. Pin the upper edge of the ruffle to the center front of the dress. Gather the ruffle by pulling a set of thread tails (either the top threads OR the bobbin threads) until the ruffle measures 5˝ long. Pin the ruffle down along the center front of the dress.

5. Press each end of the 6˝-long piece of ribbon under ½˝. Place on top of the ruffle on the dress, tucking the folded ribbon ends under the ruffle.

6. Topstitch the ribbon on top of the gathered ruffle, with the stitching line in the center of the ribbon.

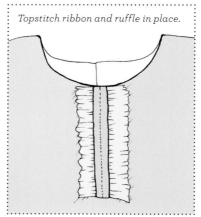

Topstitch ribbon and ruffle in place.

7. Sew the 3 buttons onto the ribbon, at 1½˝, 2½˝, and 3½˝ down from the upper finished neck edge.

Give your Little Pearl a final press and slip it onto the sweet shoulders of your little girl!

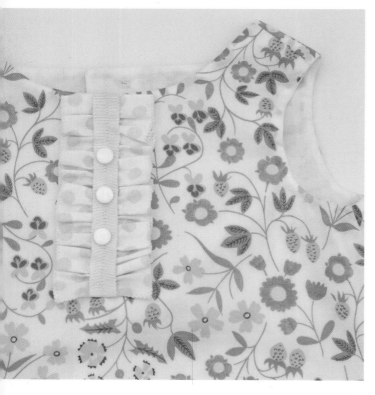

MICHELLE
MY BELLE
DRESS

MICHELLE MY BELLE DRESS

This fancy frock, sewn up in the seasonal Liberty of London print Pablo Pepper, has a nipped waist and full hemline just like my favorite vintage dress. I added a ruffled embellishment to the neckline with little pearl buttons stitched on top. I think of this as the perfect party dress—not too dressy, perfectly feminine, and so comfortable in soft Tana Lawn.

The unlined, gathered skirt will require a pretty slip. I prefer to wear a slip, which adds less bulk at the waist, rather than fully lining with another gathered layer of fabric. A beautiful vintage slip with lace edging would be perfect with this vintage-inspired dress.

Note: This dress would be fun with a contrasting waist panel to give it even more of that nipped-in look.

Supplies Needed

Refer to the ladies' size chart (page 158).

FABRIC

Ladies' X-small or Small

2 yards Liberty Tana Lawn

½ yard lining fabric (I prefer cotton voile, China silk, or rayon lining.)

1 strip 2¼″ × 14″ of fabric for contrasting ruffle

Ladies' Medium or Large

2½ yards Liberty Tana Lawn

⅞ yard lining fabric (I prefer cotton voile, China silk, or rayon lining.)

1 strip 2¼″ × 14″ of fabric for contrasting ruffle

Ladies' X-large

2½ yards Liberty Tana Lawn

1 yard lining fabric (I prefer cotton voile, China silk, or rayon lining.)

1 strip 2¼″ × 14″ of fabric for contrasting ruffle

OTHER SUPPLIES

3 pearl buttons ⅜″ in diameter

¼ yard ⅝″-wide ribbon (I prefer cotton or silk satin, rayon seam binding, or rayon grosgrain.)

1 zipper: 18″ (small or medium) OR 20″ (large or x-large)

Optional: 1 small hook and eye

Cutting

Patterns are on tissue paper pattern sheets. Refer to the cutting layout below to place the pattern pieces on the fabric. *

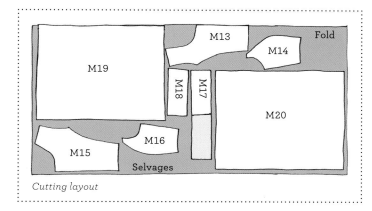

Cutting layout

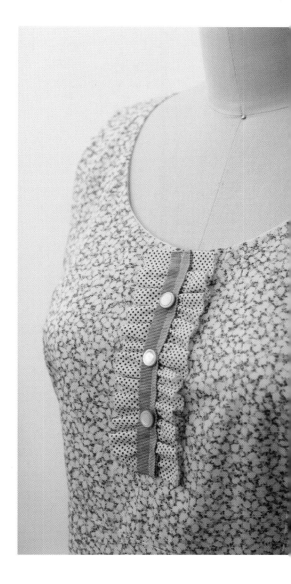

Tana Lawn Print

Cut 1 of pattern piece M13
Bodice Center Front, on fold.

Cut 2 of pattern piece M14
Bodice Side Front.

Cut 2 of pattern piece M15
Bodice Back.

Cut 2 of pattern piece M16
Bodice Side Back.

Cut 1 of pattern piece M17
Midriff Front Panel on fold. *

Cut 2 of pattern piece M18
Midriff Back Panel.

Cut 1 of pattern piece M19
Skirt Front on fold.

Cut 2 of pattern piece M20
Skirt Back.

Lining Fabric

Cut 1 of pattern piece M13
Bodice Center Front, on fold.

Cut 2 of pattern piece M14
Bodice Side Front.

Cut 2 of pattern piece M15
Bodice Back.

Cut 2 of pattern piece M16
Bodice Side Back.

Cut 1 of pattern piece M17
Midriff Front Panel, on fold.

Cut 2 of pattern piece M18
Midriff Back Panel.

* If your size M17 pattern piece will not fit on the fold, trace pattern piece right side up on a single layer of fabric, flip over along fold line, and trace the reverse in place to complete the shape as shown.

CONSTRUCTION

- *Unless otherwise indicated, use a ½″ seam allowance, sew all seams with the right sides of the fabric facing each other, and backstitch at the beginning and end of all seams.*

- *Top stitching, unless otherwise indicated, should be spaced ⅛″ away from edges or seams.*

Sew

SEW BODICE

1. Using the cotton print fabric pieces, sew the Bodice Side Front (M14) pieces onto each side of the Bodice Center Front (M13), matching notches. Clip seam allowances at curves. Press.

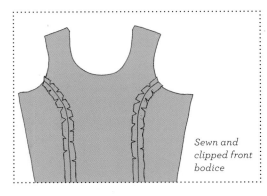

Sewn and clipped front bodice

2. Sew a Bodice Side Back (M16) piece to a Bodice Back (M15), matching notches. Clip and press. Repeat with the other pair of M16 and M15.

3. Sew the Midriff Front Panel (M17) to the lower edge of the bodice front, matching notches on midriff to the bottom of the bodice front. Press.

4. Sew a Midriff Back Panel (M18) piece to the lower edges of each bodice back, matching notches on midriff pieces to the bottoms of the bodice backs. Press.

5. Sew the bodice front to the bodice backs at the shoulder seams. Press.

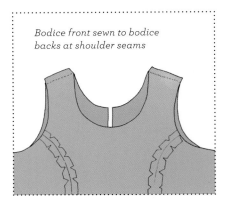

Bodice front sewn to bodice backs at shoulder seams

6. Repeat Steps 1–5 with the bodice lining pieces.

7. Staystitch the neckline edge of the outer dress pieces by sewing a row of stitching a scant ½″ from the cut neckline edge. This will prevent the neckline from stretching when the dress is turned right side out.

8. Sew the neckline edge of the dress bodice to the bodice lining.

9. Sew an armhole opening of the bodice to the bodice lining. Repeat on the other side.

10. Clip and notch curved seam allowances around neck and armhole opening. Turn the bodice right side out by pulling the back bodice sides through the shoulder seams. Press.

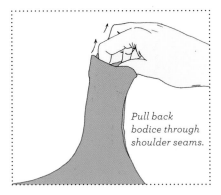

Pull back bodice through shoulder seams.

11. Sew the bodice side seams by matching the lining to the lining and the outer fabric to the outer fabric and then stitching in a single continuous seam. Press.

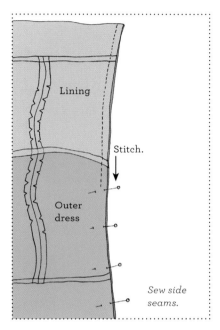

Lining

Stitch.

Outer dress

Sew side seams.

12. Staystitch the lower raw edge of the bodice on the outer dress fabric only.

SEW SKIRT

1. Sew the Skirt Back (M20) pieces to either side of the Skirt Front (M19), matching notches. Press.

2. Sew the center back skirt seam from the hem up to the zipper stop mark.

Assemble

1. Pin the skirt to the lower edge of the bodice outer fabric only, and match the center back raw edges, the center fronts, and the side seams. Pin small, irregular tucks in the skirt fabric until the skirt is the same size as the bodice. Instead of pinning in tucks, you could sew 2 rows of basting stitches around the top of the skirt and gather to match the circumference of the bodice before pinning in place.

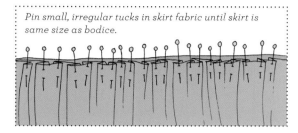

Pin small, irregular tucks in skirt fabric until skirt is same size as bodice.

2. Sew the skirt to the bodice. Press the seam allowances up toward the bodice.

3. Press the seam allowances of the bodice lining's bottom and center back edges under toward the wrong side of the dress fabric.

4. Referring to Sewing Tips, Invisible Zipper (page 24), install the zipper at the center back seam, keeping the lining free of the zipper. The pattern allows for up to a 1˝ seam allowance at the center back, so try the dress on before installing the zipper and adjust for your desired amount of ease.

5. Hand sew the center back and lower pressed edges of the lining to the zipper tape and skirt seam allowances, respectively.

6. Hem the dress ⅝˝.

Trim

1. Refer to Little Pearl Dress, Finish, Steps 3–6 (page 142), to make a 6˝-long ruffle with the 2¼˝ × 14˝ strip of fabric and 7˝-long piece of ribbon.

2. Sew the 3 buttons onto the ribbon, at 1½˝, 3˝, and 4½˝ down from the upper finished neck edge.

Optional: Hand sew a hook and eye to the upper edges of the center back opening above the zipper.

Give your frock a final press, and it's ready to wear!

LULU
TUNIC

LULU TUNIC

Hoping to draft a dress I'd want to live in, I created this simple tunic with a sheer upper bodice. The Lulu Tunic is perfect for year-round wear. Layer it in the fall and winter with tights and a comfy sweater, or wear it in the middle of summer with sandals and bare legs.

I used the seasonal Liberty of London Tana Lawn print Kyaoko, with its acid-bright colors on a black background. For the upper bodice, I used a double layer of sheer black voile with white dots.

Note: You could even make this up with two different Liberty prints, one for the dress and one for the upper bodice.

I hope this becomes a staple pattern for your sewn wardrobe.

Supplies Needed

FABRIC
Refer to the ladies' size chart (page 158).

Ladies' X-small or Small

1 yard Liberty Tana Lawn

1½ yards upper bodice fabric (I prefer cotton or silk voile, chiffon, georgette, or batiste.)

Ladies' Medium or Large

1 yard Liberty Tana Lawn

1½ yards upper bodice fabric (I prefer cotton or silk voile, chiffon, georgette, or batiste.)

Ladies' X-large

1⅛ yards Liberty Tana Lawn

1⅝ yards upper bodice fabric (I prefer cotton or silk voile, chiffon, georgette, or batiste.)

OTHER SUPPLIES
1 small hook and eye

Cutting

Patterns are on tissue paper pattern sheets. Refer to the cutting layout below to place the pattern pieces on the fabrics.

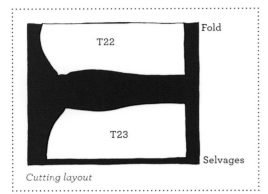

Cutting layout

Tana Lawn Print

Cut 1 of pattern piece T22 Dress Front on fold.

Cut 1 of pattern piece T23 Dress Back on fold.

Bodice Fabric

Cut 2 of pattern piece T24 Upper Bodice Front on fold (1 outer, 1 lining).

Cut 4 of pattern piece T25 Upper Bodice Back (2 outer, 2 lining).

CONSTRUCTION

- *Unless otherwise indicated, use a ½″ seam allowance, sew all seams with the right sides of the fabric facing each other, and backstitch at the beginning and end of all seams.*

- *Topstitching, unless otherwise indicated, should be spaced ⅛″ away from edges or seams.*

Note: When using sheer fabric for the upper bodice, I like to finish seams by sewing another stitching line in the seam allowance a scant ⅛″ away from the seamline and trimming the excess seam allowances just past the second stitching line.

Sew

1. Staystitch all 4 of the Upper Bodice Back pieces (T25) along the center back seamline between large dots marked on the tissue paper pattern.

2. Sew the outer fabric Upper Bodice Front (T24) to Back (T25) at the shoulder seams. Repeat with the upper bodice lining pieces.

3. Sew the outer fabric upper bodice to the upper bodice lining around the neck and sleeve edges. When you sew the neck edge, begin sewing at the center back dot, and turn and pivot at the center back neck. Continue sewing, pivot again at the opposite center back, and stop sewing at the other center back dot. Trim seam allowances and clip curved edges. Turn right side out. Press.

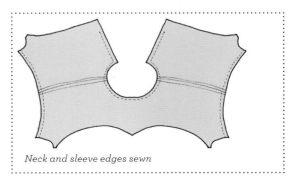

Neck and sleeve edges sewn

4. Sew the short center back seam of the upper bodice back outer pieces from the lower edge up to the dot. Clip the seam allowance edges at the small dot and stop at the stitching line. Press. Repeat with the corresponding pieces of the lining.

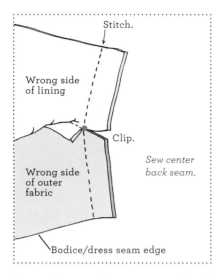

Stitch.

Wrong side of lining

Clip.

Sew center back seam.

Wrong side of outer fabric

Bodice/dress seam edge

5. Sew darts in the Dress Front (T22).

6. Match the upper bodice underarm seams, lining to lining and outer fabric to outer fabric. Sew in a single continuous seam. Trim seam allowances. Press.

7. Sew the dress front to the dress back at the side seams. Press.

8. Sew the lower edge of the upper dress bodice to the upper edge of the dress. Press the seam allowances down toward the lower dress. Topstitch the seam on the lower dress side, stitching through the outer fabric and seam allowances all the way around the dress.

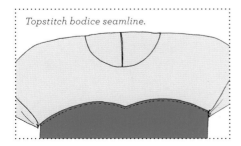

Topstitch bodice seamline.

9. Hem the dress ⅝˝.

10. Sew the hook and eye onto the inside back neck edge of the dress. Sew the hook to the right side of the opening (as it is worn) and the eye to the left side of the opening.

Hook and eye sewn inside dress

After a final press, the tunic is ready to wear. Whether you're headed to work or for a special night out, I hope this dress makes you feel beautiful.

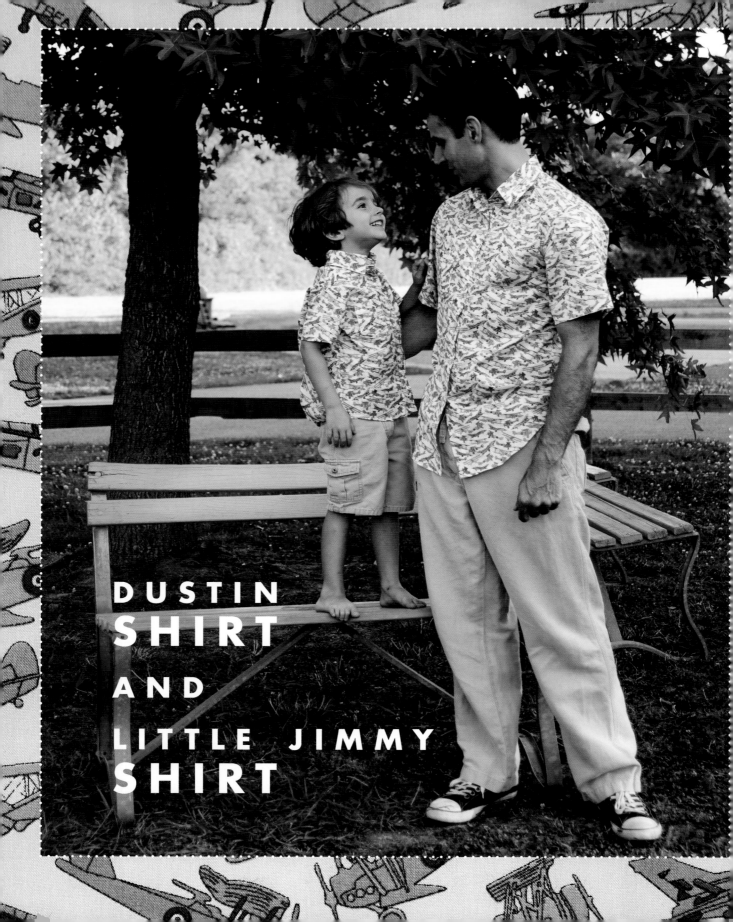

DUSTIN
SHIRT
AND
LITTLE JIMMY
SHIRT

Because every man, no matter what age, needs a classic Liberty shirt, I created this collared, short-sleeved, button-front shirt. I chose to make both versions in the seasonal Liberty of London print Tom's Jet because of the vintage feel, but a classic floral would also be so very handsome. With the soft hand of Tana Lawn, this will be the most comfortable collared shirt in the closet—surely a first pick whenever the closet door is opened.

Supplies Needed

Refer to the boys' and men's size charts (page 158).

FABRIC

Boys

X-small (3/4) or Small (5/6)
⅞ yard Liberty Tana Lawn

Medium (7/8)
1¼ yard Liberty Tana Lawn

Large (9/10)
1½ yards Liberty Tana Lawn

Men

Small or Medium
1¾ yards Liberty Tana Lawn

Large or X-large
2½ yards Liberty Tana Lawn

OTHER SUPPLIES

Boys

7 pearl buttons, ⅜˝ in diameter
....
¾ yard lightweight fusible interfacing, 20˝ wide*
....

Men

9 pearl buttons, ⁷⁄₁₆˝ in diameter
....
1 yard lightweight fusible interfacing, 20˝ wide*
....

* *(I use Pellon Bi-Stretch Lite)*

Cutting

Patterns are on tissue paper pattern sheets. Boys' size pattern piece numbers are prefaced with J, and Men's sizes by D. Refer to the cutting layouts below to place the pattern pieces on the fabric.

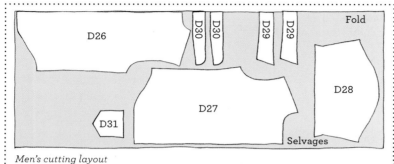

Men's cutting layout

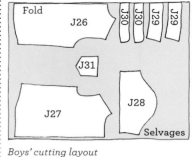

Boys' cutting layout

Tana Lawn Print

Cut 1 of pattern piece 26 Shirt Back on fold.

Cut 2 of pattern piece 27 Shirt Front.

Cut 2 of pattern piece 28 Sleeve.

Cut 2 of pattern piece 29 Collar on fold.

Cut 2 of pattern piece 30 Collar Stand on fold.

Cut 2 of pattern piece 31 Pocket.

Lightweight Fusible Interfacing

TIP *Do not fold interfacing. Instead, trace collar pieces right side up, flip pattern pieces over along fold line, and trace the other half in place.*

Cut 1 of pattern piece 29 Collar.

Cut 1 of pattern piece 30 Collar Stand.

Cut 2 strips 1˝ wide (boys') or 1¼˝ wide (men's) × the length of the center front of the shirt size you are making.

CONSTRUCTION

- *Unless otherwise indicated, use a ½˝ seam allowance, sew all seams with the right sides of the fabric facing each other, and backstitch at the beginning and end of all seams.*

- *Topstitching, unless otherwise indicated, should be spaced ⅛˝ away from edges or seams.*

Sew

SEW COLLAR AND COLLAR STAND

1. Fuse the Collar interfacing (29) to the wrong side of a Collar (29) piece. This is now the outer collar. Fuse the Collar Stand interfacing (30) to the wrong side of a Collar Stand (30) piece. This is now the outer collar stand.

2. Sew the inner and outer collar pieces together along the short sides and long upper edge. Clip away excess seam allowances. Turn right side out. Press.

TIP *To get nice collar points, stop sewing about 1/16˝ from the corner, pivot, take two stitches on the diagonal, pivot, and continue sewing the collar. When clipping the excess seam allowances at the point, clip just outside the diagonal stitching line and at each leg of the seam, tapering the seam allowance to the corner.*

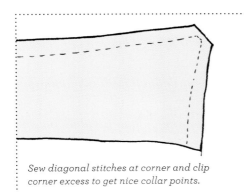

Sew diagonal stitches at corner and clip corner excess to get nice collar points.

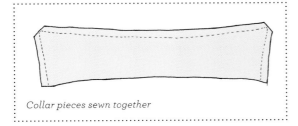

Collar pieces sewn together

3. Topstitch the finished edges of the collar.

4. Matching the collar stand notches to the finished edges of the collar, sandwich the finished collar between the outer and inner collar stands, with the inner collar stand facing the outer (right) side of the collar. Sew the 2 collar stand upper edges together, trapping the lower, unfinished edge of the collar in the seam. Trim the seam allowances and turn right side out. Press.

5. Turn up the inner collar stand seam allowance along the lower, unfinished edge.

SEW POCKET

1. Sew the Pocket (31) pieces together all the way around, leaving a 1½˝ opening along the upper edge. Clip the excess seam allowance at the corners and turn right side out.

2. Topstitch the upper finished pocket edge, closing the seam opening with the seam allowances pressed to the inside of the pocket.

Note: I think it looks nice to sew two rows of top stitching here, one just below the edge and another about 3/8˝ down for boys' sizes, or 1˝ for men's sizes.

3. Topstitch the pocket side and lower edges to the left shirt front at the pocket placement lines indicated on the pattern piece. To mimic the optional 2 rows of stitching in Step 2, sew 2 rows of top stitching here, the first just inside the edge and the other about ¼˝ from the edge.

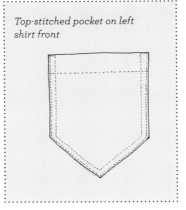

Top-stitched pocket on left shirt front

Assemble

1. Press the front placket edge of each Shirt Front (27) to the wrong side along the fold line indicated on the pattern piece. Align each of the fusible interfacing strips to the pressed fold line with the fusible side facing the wrong side of the fabric. Fuse in place.

2. Press the folded edge under again, pressing the cut raw edge to the existing crease.

3. Topstitch the pressed edge of the placket facing section to the Shirt Front.

4. Sew the Shirt Fronts to the Shirt Back (28) at the shoulder seams. Press.

5. Sew the sleeves to the shirt, matching notches. Press. Notch and trim the seam allowances along the curved edges.

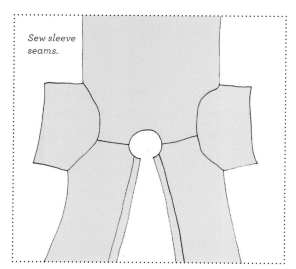

Sew sleeve seams.

6. Sew the shirt side and sleeve seams in a single continuous seamline. Press.

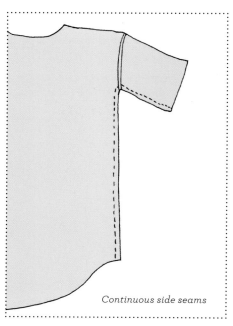

Continuous side seams

7. Sew the outer collar stand to the shirt neck edge, keeping the inner collar stand free of the seam. Clip and notch the seam allowances and press them up into the collar stand. Pin the pressed, inside collar stand to the outer collar stand with wrong sides together. Topstitch the collar stand perimeter. Note: The neck edge seam allowances should now be trapped inside the collar stand.

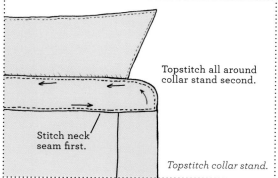

Topstitch all around collar stand second.

Stitch neck seam first.

Topstitch collar stand.

SEW BUTTONHOLES AND BUTTONS

1. Sew 6 (boys) or 8 (men) buttonholes in the left shirt front, the first horizontal on the collar stand and the rest vertical, down the front placket. For placement, mark the buttonholes according to the pattern piece.

2. Sew the buttons to the right Shirt Front. Follow the pattern piece for placement. Sew the remaining button 2˝ below the lowest button. This is an extra in case a button comes off and gets lost!

HEM SLEEVES AND SHIRT

1. Turn up the total sleeve hem allowance to the wrong side. Press. Fold the raw edge of the hem allowance down to the creased edge,encasing it in the fold, and press again. Topstitch the sleeve hem along the second pressed fold of the hem. Refer to your sewing machine manual to utilize the free-arm feature of the machine if it is offered.

2. Hem the lower edge of the shirt ½˝.

Press or starch the shirt, and it is ready to sport. Wouldn't a matching shirt on a father and son be so handsome for a family portrait!

SIZE CHART

These body measurements are guidelines to help you choose the correct pattern size. Each garment includes wearing/design ease to ensure that it fits as designed.

Measure the pattern pieces and subtract seam allowances to find out the finished garment dimensions. Compare these dimensions with your measurements; and be sure the finished garment is larger than your actual measurements. For a fitted style, finished measurements should be around 1″ larger in the bust/chest. For a less fitted style, measurements should be around 3″ larger (or more) in the bust/chest.

Sometimes I use the measurements of a favorite garment, one similar to the pattern I am making, to determine the finished measurements.

Measurements are listed in inches.

LADIES

Size	XS 0/2	S 4/6	M 8/10	L 12/14	XL 16
Bust	32–33½	34–35½	36–37½	38–40½	42–43½
Natural waist	25–26	27–28	29–30	31–33	34–36
Hip	34–36	37–38	39–40	41–43	44–46

MEN

Size	S	M	L	XL
Chest	35–37	38–40	41–43	44–46
Waist	29–31	32–34	35–38	38–40
Neck	14½	15½	16½	17½

INFANTS/TODDLERS

Size	XS 12–18 mo	S 18–24 mo	M 3	L 4
Height	29–31	32–35	36–39	39–42
Weight (pounds)	22–27	27–30	30–34	34–39
Chest	19½	20½	21½	22½
Waist	19	20	21	21½

BOYS

Size	XS 3/4	S 5/6	M 7/8	L 9/10
Height	37–42	43–47	48–53	54–57
Weight (pounds)	34–40	41–50	51–70	71–82
Chest	21–23	24–25	25–27	27–28
Waist	21–22	22–23	23–24	24–25

RESOURCES

Fabric and Supplies

Liberty of London
Regent Street
London W1B 5AH
+44 (0) 20 7734 1234

liberty.co.uk

Purl Soho
459 Broome Street
New York, NY 10013
(212) 420-8796

purlsoho.com

superbuzzy
1794 East Main Street
Ventura, CA 93001
(805) 643-4143

superbuzzy.com

Shaukat & Company
170-172 Old Brompton
Road
London SW5 0BA
+44 (0) 20 7373 6927

shaukat.co.uk

Tillycharles
etsy.com/shop/
tillycharles

Textile Fabric Store
2717 Franklin Pike
Nashville, TN 37204
(615) 297-5346

textilefabricstore.com

The City Quilter
133 West 25th Street
New York, NY 10001
(212) 807-0390

cityquilter.com

Seattle Fabrics
8702 Aurora Avenue
North
Seattle, WA 98103
(866) 925-0670

seattlefabrics.com

B. Black and Sons
548 South Los Angeles
Street
Los Angeles, CA 90013
(800) 433-1546

bblackandsons.com

Moda Fabrics
Wholesale

unitednotions.com

FreeSpirit Fabrics
Wholesale

freespiritfabric.com

Steinlauf and Stoller Inc.
239 West 39th St.
New York, NY 10018
(212) 869-0321

steinlaufandstoller.com

The Warm Company
Wholesale
(425) 248-2424

warmcompany.com

Paper Pieces
paperpieces.com

For Your Sewing and Quilting Library

All-in-One Quilter's Reference Tool; Harriet Hargrave, Sharyn Craig, Alex Anderson, Liz Aneloski; C&T Publishing

Heirloom Machine Quilting: A Comprehensive Guide to Hand-Quilting Effects Using Your Sewing Machine, 4th Edition; Harriet Hargrave; C&T Publishing

The New Complete Guide to Sewing: Step-by-Step Techniques for Making Clothes and Home Accessories, Updated Edition with All-New Projects and Simplicity Patterns; Reader's Digest

High-Fashion Sewing Secrets from the World's Best Designers: A Step-by-Step Guide to Sewing Stylish Seams, Buttonholes, Pockets, Collars, Hems, and More; Claire B. Shaeffer; Rodale Books

Threads Sewing Guide: A Complete Reference from America's Best-Loved Sewing Magazine; Carol Fresia, ed.; Taunton Press

ABOUT THE AUTHOR

Alexia Marcelle Abegg was born in Folsom, California, on the day Mount St. Helens erupted in Washington—May 18, 1980. She has been inspired by her mother's and father's creativity and dedication to art throughout her life.

An award-winning designer, artist, and writer, Alexia has always been fascinated with the art of sewing. She studied fashion and fine arts in college.

After trying her hand at photography, production, acting, costuming, hair and makeup for film and television, fashion design, and custom sewing, she found her home in creating fine art quilts and sewing patterns while living in Brooklyn, New York. She later worked for esteemed designer Anna Maria Horner in Nashville, Tennessee, which cemented her love for the sewing and quilting world.

Alexia and her artist husband, Rob Bancroft, live in Nashville with their two dogs. She currently divides her time among creating patterns for their company, Green Bee Design and Patterns; teaching; making art; and writing.